A Mile Wide
and
An Inch Deep

America's Shallow
Approach to Adolescence

Essays on Adolescent Metaphors,
Figures of Speech, Plays on Words,
Concepts and Other Ways to Better
Understand Adolescents and Adolescence

Bret Stephenson MA

ISBN-13: 978-1546518082

ISBN-10: 1546518088

Text design and layout by Bret Stephenson
This book was typeset in Palatino Lynotype with Hypatia Sans Pro and Calibri used as highlight typefaces
Cover design by Bret Stephenson

Author of:

From Boys to Men: Spiritual Rites of Passage in an Indulgent Age

The Undercurrents of Adolescence: Tracking the Evolution of Modern Adolescence and Delinquency Through Classic Cinema

DEDICATION

This book is dedicated to the many wonderful adult youth workers, counselors, therapists, probation officers, parents, and others who have crossed my path during this journey through the world of adolescence. You have taught me so many ways to engage with this fascinating clientele, and left me with many intriguing memories.

One of my goals for this book it to help the next generation of people helping teens get a better grasp on the adolescent process. Be curious, be inventive, be passionate. Be congruent in what you say versus what you actually do. Don't blindly follow old dogma and practices that don't work. Experiment. Have fun. Cry once in a while at the sad stories and even sadder outcomes that invariably come.

Get good at this work and then pass what you've learned to the generation following you.

I leave you with this favorite quote of mine. When you are following a pre-defined 'program' that doesn't fit your client's needs, when developing your own approaches and models, keep this in mind regarding Treatment vs Prevention:

Why is there never enough time to do it right, but always enough time to do it over again?

Bret Stephenson

CONTENTS

Introduction

Bret Stephenson

Introduction

When I first began my career with teens almost 30 years ago, much of the literature I could find on adolescence was of the self-help variety for parents. The content was largely about controlling teens. So much of the available literature was about teen behavior as something to be avoided and fixed, if possible. Indeed, many youth workers I know agree that adolescence is actually being pathologized in the US, something that needs a cure and hopefully a quick, simple fix. It only took me a few years to realize that adolescent rebellious behavior serves a number of purposes, and trying to stop this amazing growth process only causes more harm than it helps.

I learned that adolescence provides a great service to the overall community by questioning the status quo, keeping us adults on our toes, and reflecting back to us the way teens perceive the world. Teens are a cultural mirror, one of my main working metaphors. One of their important roles is to 'reflect' back at us how they view things. It is our job to listen, fix what should be fixed, and help explain how some things are just life and not in anyone's control without trying to kill their idealism and dreams.

I also learned that it was more productive to try and work on the issues *creating* alleged teen problems like fatherlessness, life with single moms, declining school health, changing societal values and so on. And then there are the literal problems teens face: gangs, drugs, underage sex, violence, poor school performance, bullying and more. As I came to understand all these dynamics better and deeper, I struggled to find ways to explain the understanding I was developing to other people.

I came up with a few metaphors like the cultural mirror above that helped people see the subtleties of the adolescent world. Occasionally I would hear an interesting phrase, or a figure of speech that I could also use to adapt my material and information into. Putting a mental image to behavior helped parents and other youth workers better understand the underestimated role teens play in any culture.

In my first book, *From Boys to Men: Spiritual Rites of Passage in an Indulgent Age* I spent a lot of time explaining the rite of passage/initiation process that is/was inherent to most cultures worldwide. Communities all over the world, separated by vast distances, diverse beliefs and little outside communication, all developed a process for helping teen boys and girls grow into healthy men and women. To use another metaphor, rites of passage (ROPs) were the glue that held small communities together, ritualizing the growth process to a degree that full community celebrations supported the youths' efforts to grow. In a masterful reframe of the old adage "It takes a village..." my friend and mentor David Blumenkrantz states that "It takes a *whole* child to raise a [healthy] village." Healthy children are the barometer of a community's health.

Letting go of these processes in favor of "civilization" has been most damaging to modern teens, and subsequently to our community health multiple generations later. My second book, *The Undercurrents of Adolescence: Tracking the Evolution of Modern Adolescence and Delinquency Through Classic Cinema*, took a deep look at the creation and invention of modern adolescence in the 20th century. And I do mean the actual *invention* of what we know today. After painting a picture of American societal changes during the Industrial Revolution, we see the dramatic changes that shifting from a rural culture to an urban one did to teens. Add a bunch of "civilized" approaches and laws and teens have never been the same.

Adolescence is the second greatest growth phase we ever go through, second only to birth-to-two years old. Over just a couple of years, teens radically change body shapes and sizes, their perception of the world and their role in it, they begin breaking away from the family, create a stronger attachment to peers, and acquire a taste for more adult behavior. They are sexually capable and active. They experiment with other behaviors that scare us adults and parents but that we likely indulged in to some degree ourselves in our own youth.

But what seems to bother most people about adolescence is its testing process, which many people refer to as defiant or rebellious behavior. I don't think that is completely accurate, at least in early adolescence. It is not that teens begin by merely flouting the rules, but it's more about them needing to see if the reality they have been taught as children really stands up to testing. They need to prove for themselves the ways of the world. If guided, as in a rite of passage model, then the testing is met with healthy resistance and accommodation, helping teens come to adult conclusions about the world and their role in it. For example, I believe teens start shifting into adulthood when they learn the difference between the idealistic teen hope of the way the world *should* be versus the way *it actually is*. The trick is not to burst all their dreams and goals, and also not to squelch their curiosity and subsequent growth from their behavior and experiences. After all, don't we learn our deepest and most important lessons from our mistakes? If we stop teens from being able to experiment and push the boundaries a bit, we deny them this growth opportunity.

Of course boundaries and consequences around their behavior have to happen to keep teens from getting too far out of control, but we must stop pathologizing teens for testing those boundaries. They are not wrong or bad by simple virtue of testing our norms and values. Too many people misunderstand the need to test and learn with some alleged plot against adults and parents to just be defiant and devious for fun. It may seem, or feel like that, but it is a necessary process. Since we all know that we learn many of our most important life lessons through our mistakes, we have to allow them enough room to slip and grow without totally shutting down their ability to experiment a bit.

Adolescents serve a greater function in society than most adults realize. For much of the past hundred years, teens have been made more and more irresponsible, which now many adults sadly hold that irresponsibility against teens. The attempt of this book is to give the reader a wide variety of ways to understand and think about the process and challenge of adolescence. My goal has been to give you numerous ways to ponder this incredible developmental period, too often misunderstood.

This book has about 20 different ways of looking at adolescents in particular, and adolescence in general. My hope it to put this complicated yet crucial process into simple terms and images that help people have better interactions and relationships with teens, who in spite of all their crazy behavior, need us to understand why they do what they do.

One

Canaries in the Coal Mine

Teenagers, especially girl ones, seem like the perfect canary-in-the-coal-mine characters to me. They capture American culture and its perversion, its hypocrisy - how absorbed we are with youth and beauty and sexualized imagery, for instance, while preaching abstinence and modesty.
Antonya Nelson

Accounts vary, but for at least a hundred years or more miners in the past took canaries into the mines with them to act as a low-tech warning mechanism that dangerous gases were present. Canaries were susceptible to low amounts of methane and other gases that were harmful or even fatal to human miners. When England phased out canaries in mines in 1986, miners grieved over the loss of these cheerful birds that represented both life and death. Apparently, high-tech monitors and sensors did not create the same relationship as watching another living thing.

For me, adolescents are canaries in the coal mine of modern culture. After 29 years with thousands of teens from all walks of life I have come to believe that like those canaries who were floundering in a gas-infected mine, our teens are not faring so well in modern times. The problem is we are not caring for them in their struggle, and often blame them for many of society's ills rather than see teens for the symptom of a larger problem they represent.

In my first book, *From Boys to Men,* I spent a fair amount of time offering up scores of statistics to show the reader how difficult and often dangerous it is for modern teens. Some people felt I went too heavy on the stats, depressing readers with fact after fact about teen violence, drug use, school failure, pregnancy, gangs and so on. Other authors similarly document how difficult it is for modern teens, such as Kindlon and Thompson's *Raising Cain: Protecting the Emotional Life of Boys,* Blankenhorn's *Fatherless America: Confronting Our Most Urgent Social Problem,* Kipnis' *Angry Young Men: How Parents, Teachers, and Counselors Can Help "Bad Boys" Become Good Men,* and Garbarino's *Lost Boys: Why Our Sons Turn Violent and How We Can Save Them,* to name a few. The Internet has made finding sad statistics easy.

Rather than try to convince you about how difficult it is for modern teens, I'm going to trust that you have a sense of this from your local stories and news, from more and more school problems and a growing number of gangs. What's amazing is that so many teens surf the turbulent waters of modern life so well, but sadly many do not.

Canaries in a coal mine was one of the first metaphors I really pondered related to teens. As I tried more and more often to explain to adults I was working with why teens act certain ways, I searched for ways to help make what I knew to be true about teens more understandable. Indeed, this book is a product of that effort to find multiple, diverse and deep ways to explain the process of adolescence as I have come to understand it.

So why, or how, are teens vulnerable canaries in the dangerous coal mine of modern society? Because they are exposed to a declining moral and family structure. We continue with a divorce rate of about 50%, and 60% failure for second marriages. More than half the kids in America live in a single parent home. School performance has been dwindling for years in spite of, or perhaps due to, the quest to standardize education. Teens are now exposed to more violence than at any earlier time. Designer drugs are rampant, such as meth and OxyContin. Youth regularly sell or trade their psychotropic prescription drugs like Ritalin or Seroquel to other kids to abuse. There are reportedly almost 1,000,000 gang members in the US, about half of them teens with that number growing and spreading to other countries.

Modern teens have to navigate these obstacles and temptations, which is more to ask than teens of the 1950's or earlier. Depression now commonly begins in early adolescence rather than adulthood. The list of mental health problems associated with teens (and other ages) include ADD/ADHD, eating disorders, bipolar disorder, conduct disorders, oppositional defiant disorder, intermittent explosive disorder, reactive attachment disorder, suicide and post-traumatic stress disorder, fetal alcohol effects and syndrome. Suicide is the third-leading cause of death for 15- to 24-year-olds in America, according to the U.S. Centers for Disease Control and Prevention (CDC), surpassed only by accidents and homicide. Looked at another way, teens will most likely die from driving and drinking, being murdered or by killing themselves.

Did the teens from the 1950's or the 1800's have to ponder these common ways of dying? Would, or did they have all of these mental problems? Would they have needed acronyms (like ADD/ADHD, OCD, RAD, ODD, FAE/FAS)? Were they worse off without such diagnoses? Was my hyperactive brother really ADHD and was he somehow underserved by not having a fancy diagnosis in the 1960s? How come no one remembers all of this youth drama in earlier generations, and are we all better off for the plethora of mental health services, counseling agencies, boot camps, juvenile halls, group-homes, alternative schools, and residential treatment centers? My experience says no.

Was this gauntlet of risk factors caused by teens or have they inherited them as obstacles to avoid or overcome from us adults? Did teens change or did times change? What will youth culture be like in another 20 or 50 years?

OK, I'm guilty of getting on my soapbox and taking a few moments to paint a picture, a not very pretty picture. We all have complaints in our jobs. My complaint is that there are not enough good programs or projects that understand how adolescence works, that teens are too often considered at fault for not doing better in an ever-changing culture that seems to be getting more dangerous and dysfunctional. In my job, failure often means kids die, either on the streets or at their own hand. They self-destruct in gangs or from drugs. Their lack of motivation to join our adult club sabotages their education efforts. Many end up in jail or prison as adults.

Quite simply, teens are not faring well. Not all of them, of course, but far too many. If we look at teens as canaries in a coal mine, litmus paper, a barometer, scorecard, or any other comparison, we'll find too many are looking a little ragged. As a collective, cultural group, our teen canaries are floundering in their cages in dangerous mines. The question for me, for all of us, is whether we will notice their condition and remove them from their toxic environment. Will we pull them from the mine in time or wait to see if they are merely sick or going to die? What does their lack of life energy and overall health tell us?

Two

The Zen of Adolescence

Change will not come if we wait for some other person or some other time. We are the ones we've been waiting for. We are the change that we seek.
Barack Obama

If a teen dies in the street, does he make a sound if there's no one there to hear him? This is a graphic variation of the classic Zen koan, or teaching: If a tree falls in the forest does it make a sound if there is no one there to hear it. I've always loved pondering these abstract concepts in my personal pursuit to grow and change. Often, teens will enjoy them as mental exercises as well. Adolescence is usually the shifting, developmentally, from the typically concrete "either/or", "black/white" all or nothing tendency of young teens to the ability to grasp more abstract concepts: the gray area of everyday life.

I don't pretend to be fluent in the Zen traditions, but to me they reflect a deep understanding of how things are interrelated, how big lessons can be learned from small things, and that there is more than one way to look at a topic.

For me, adolescence has been the best teacher, best therapy I ever had. Thousands of teens later I've had to look at everything I believe, or believed to be true. I was forced to look at my own father issues repeatedly, or my deteriorated relationship with my brother. I had to look at politics, cultural changes before I was born, the media and countless other dynamics that affect kids every day. I had to get over my false assumptions about what teens are about and how they should be. After all, I began working with teens before I was a dad, so what frame of reference did I have for how parents should behave or what I had learned from my own parents?

The "tree falls in the forest..." koan is about the understanding that we change what we observe, also a rule in quantum physics. When we see a tree fall, it makes a big thud as it hits the ground. But how can we be sure it still does if we're far away? The point and fact is we can't. We have to get close enough to hear it one way or the other, even electronically.

Gary Larsen, who amused us for years with his *Far Side* cartoons was brilliant at this, showing us cattle that discuss politics or physics when no humans are watching. When humans happen to drive by the pasture, the cows back to chewing their cuds and acting stupid, as we expect of them. But once the people had passed, the cows went back to standing on their hind legs and talking intelligently with each other when no one was watching. The reality that seems to bother a lot of people, metaphorically, is what do the cows (or teens) actually do when no one is looking? And if the environment is not conducive to sharing, like the cows, teens will also hide their behavior from our view.

Those of us who observe teens seem to understand these limitations. I can't always observe the teens I work with. I can hope I know what they do when out of sight but I can't be sure, because they have to tell me (or not). Is she being good or safe when no adults are watching? Did he really do what I heard he did? I try to teach that integrity is how a person behaves when no one is watching.

What is the deepest understanding of adolescence I can attain? Somebody once asked Einstein how he first went about testing his theories and ideas. He explained that the very first thing he did was ask himself one question: How would God have designed adolescence? That is one of the driving concepts behind my work with teens. What does adolescence look like the way God (or whoever is running the universe) planned it. Did the original model include the need for juvenile detention, boot camps, residential treatment centers, or mood altering medications? Apparently not, since all of those have been invented in the past few generations and were not needed in older cultures who dealt with adolescence successfully for thousands of years, or even America 50 years ago.

A lot of people in my career have told me what they think teens need. Interestingly, these are often people who have never had children or teens, or have never worked with adolescents. After much thought about the matter I came to believe that such comments were actually describing the way people thought or *hoped* the process should be. Countless people have remarked to me that the government must do something, that they pay their taxes so these problems of gang-banging, selling drugs, stealing cars and so on should be stopped. Obviously so, but history has shown us that punishment is not very productive, and to really fix these problems is to *prevent* them in the first place.

These types of people operate from the viewpoint of how they believe teens "should" be, without breathing through the way teens really are or what the teen process is about. I find that the less people know about the process of adolescence the more rigid their belief about how teens should be treated. People who know teens and even better, adolescence, come to see how the way it should be and the way it is are worlds apart. Ironically, this is very similar to the dynamic I described a few minutes ago about how teens evolve from the idealism of adolescence to the realism of adulthood.

Each generation of politicians claims to be stronger on crime than their weaker predecessors. A hundred or thousand mayors and district attorneys later, are we any safer walking down the street? Sadly, this tendency is, for me, representative of saying what people want to hear even if it is known the approach won't work. Too many adults have relinquished their responsibility to get personally involved by hoping in the solutions of the government, trusting the System to take care of everything. It takes a village to raise a child, not a bureaucracy. It takes the combined efforts of all the adults, not just paid youth workers, to raise a healthy child. Looked at another way, it takes a "whole child" to raise a village. Yes, we can learn from our youth. And we should...

It's clear to me the System understands very little about the Zen of Adolescence. Twenty years and a billion dollars later they keep hoping idealistically that Just Say NO will keep American kids from doing drugs. Many, many programs built for youth are based on adult logic, what we think should work based on our grownup thinking and logic. But when did teens or their behavior ever make sense? How often is what they do illogical and leaves us scratching our heads? One of the first things I really came to understand in working with teens is that I have to leave my adult logic at home. It only serves to frustrate the teens I work with, and myself, if I adhere to it blindly.

People invariably bring their own beliefs and desires into the field. Sometimes this is good, other times not. I worked for an agency a long time ago that had received funding for a new program targeting fatherless boys called Mothers and Sons. It was a pretty good model, well written and thought out; a rarity in my experience. The basic philosophy was to help single moms on one hand while helping the fatherless boys on the other.

The model called for two sets of adults to work with the kids. There would be a male and female therapist, older and experienced, kind of like an archetypal mom & dad or maybe grandma and grandpa. Next, a younger set of male and female youth workers would be used for the more experiential activities with the boys: field trips, hikes, swimming, etc. The younger team was more like an archetypal older brother and sister, or maybe auntie and uncle. Both mothers and sons would receive individual, group and family counseling services, along with the more experiential activities for the boys.

Every organization has a set of family roles of dynamics running within it, functional or dysfunctional. The head boss may be like an endearing father figure, a rich auntie like Oprah or much less functional. Our agency director was, in essence, a single mother who hated the role. She relinquished decision-making and avoided conflict resolution like a mom worn down from years of hardship. Sadly her teen son had been killed in an auto accident and this understandably affected her views on things.

In her own belief that fatherless boys needed LESS fathering and more mothering, she altered the project to suit her own beliefs. The first role she eliminated was the older counselor father figure. Thus, a model designed for fatherless boys to have older male attention was altered to adjust to her own issues of more femininity for the boys. The program never worked as designed and tested offering a father figure for the boys.

I recently did some work for an organization serving hundreds of disadvantaged teens in a variety of settings. On one hand they do an admirable job with highly resistant teens who more often than not do not want to change. Staff turnover is high, partially due to the slow results common with resistant teens. The organization provides enough pre-service training to fulfill the legal requirements, but nowhere in the company is there any information on adolescent development, family roles and so on. There are no books to read, no trainings to attend.

Basically they teach the behavioral program and they teach staff how to run the program. An analogy would be that the program is a steamroller and they teach how to drive the steam roller, but the staff/drivers have no idea what they are driving on or why. They continue to drive the program at the kids, getting mediocre results, not understanding much about the adolescent process, and usually blaming the teens for the lack of progress. Small wonder for the high staff turnover with low results and job enjoyment. They claim a ridiculously high recidivism rate that is mostly fueled by the lack of feedback they hear back from former clients as no further legal troubles have been reported. Once these kids go off probation, or simply move to another county, they fall off the grid for follow-up efforts.

I find it frustrating that the company offers no information about the product they deal with: high-risk teens. There is no resource library to borrow books from; no movies to watch. Staff blindly drive the program while never really knowing why some things work and others do not. They do not understand adolescents in particular or adolescence in general. They know Cognitive Behavioral Therapy, Anger Replacement Therapy, and other limited and uncreative Evidence Based Programs—the current trend in youth care.

While spending a couple of years trying to find an agent and/or publisher for *From Boys to Men: Spiritual Rites of Passage in an Indulgent Age*, I was repeatedly told that the book was not a parenting book. I pointed out that the bookstores were full of "how-to" books on teens and not much seemed to be getting any better in the US. People, I told them, were curious why such how-to books were not working as planned, why gangs were growing and how that was so. Why was behavior change not curing the problem? I kept reminding them that much of my work is about the cause of adolescent problems, how we went from a country with no need of group homes, residential treatment centers, juvenile detention or boot camps to a country inundated with them. If we do not understand the problem, how can we truly ever expect to fix the problem?

The Zen of Adolescence is about understanding all aspects of the adolescent process. This book is an attempt to explain in dozens of different ways how to successfully work and live with teens, how to breathe through their actions and antics, and most importantly, why they do what they do and what is normally expected of them. This book is about the *philosophy* of adolescence. Until we do that no amount of how-to books will force teens to do as we say. Adolescence is built to rebel against authority. The more we squeeze the more they rebel. We need to work with the process more and against it less.

There is another Zen proverb I'm reminded of: "Water which is too pure, has no fish." The world cannot be a perfect place. The world of teens will be chaotic at times, and challenging most of the time, but necessary for individual growth. If we keep the process too 'pure,' if we make sure the water is completely sterilized, nothing will grow in it, especially our youth.

Bret Stephenson

Three

The Drug of Distraction

The age in which we live, this non-stop distraction, is making it more impossible for the young generation to ever have the curiosity or discipline... because you need to be alone to find out anything.
Vivienne Westwood

Many of the thousands of teens I've worked with have had addiction problems. When I mention addiction problems, most people understandably think about drugs and/or alcohol, and of course this is too frequently true. However, more and more each year I look at the teen propensity to "distract" as having reached addiction levels. Of course, it doesn't help that teens see most adults nowadays with their faces buried in their phones or tablets, becoming more and more obsessed with social media, which has been described to me as "being alone together."

Countless parents have remarked to me how their teens are obsessed with PlayStation, Xbox or role playing on-line games. Often, these parental complaints revolve around the inordinate amount of time teens spend playing such games. An interesting side note to me is how so many of these parents have explained how they feel negatively toward these distractions, yet continue to purchase or otherwise support them anyway. Too many parents have admitted buying the newest version of Xbox for Christmas, only to complain later how much time their kids spend playing it. You really do have the choice to not buy the game. If your teen really wants it, let them earn it in some fashion and put logical usage boundaries on how much time they spend playing.

Most people I know admit they watch too much television, especially when I comment how I haven't watched daily TV in almost 30 years. We end up having some interesting conversations about how their time could be more productive or fun elsewhere, or the growing lack of quality programming versus more and more channels, yet I've never known anyone to actually pull the plug after discussing it. Ever.

I understand this addiction to distraction that so many of us have because I, too, have a good dose of it. A large reason I don't allow TV in my house is because I'm a total TV junkie, a product of being planted in front of the tube as a kid in the 60's. But I recall how my blue-collar parents often went to other peoples' houses for entertainment, before TV got us all totally hooked. Parents played croquet on summer evenings, card games or even board games to pass the time. Also, I've always found the growing amount of TV commercials too distracting from the show's content. We played a lot of sports and enjoyed the open Nevada desert.

When I was a kid commercials came on about every 20 minutes or so. Nowadays, they come every 8-12 minutes and account for approximately one fourth of the entire time in front of the screen. One of the major reasons I stopped watching pro sports a long time ago was when the National Football League stopped going to commercials during a natural break in the game's play and began stopping the game at regular, scheduled intervals to allow for advertisements. I quickly noticed a change in the feel of a televised game.

I remember anxiously waiting for and watching the autumn premiere of the TV show *Bonanza* because it was the only show to be run entirely with the commercials saved until the end. This dynamic was instrumental, I believe, for how quickly we adopted HBO and other premium channels that don't use regular commercials within the show.

When my wife and I first moved to Hawaii early in our relationship, our furniture got lost in transit for about two months and we similarly did more productive or engaging activities at night. When I first met my wife, she did not have TV and I felt myself falling prey to withdrawals, particularly when I was alone in her house. We spent the cold winter making presents for people, which was fun.

Teachers have thanked me for raising my own daughter without television, describing a higher than average imagination and a full attention span, among other things. Many adults worried that missing out on whatever was currently en vogue for viewing would somehow socially deprive my daughter. With modern access to the Internet, I didn't worry that she would be sheltered too much, but that I could only shelter her so long before all the media found her.

As a person who has looked at modern culture through the lenses of how older societies did things, particularly dealing with adolescents, I'm obviously reminded that TV is a product of the second half of the twentieth century and not a historical and cultural norm throughout history. TV, and many of its technological offshoots are modern drugs that have taken much of our culture by the throats, or eyes, and refused to let go.

The Drug of Distraction is not just about TV or video games, although those are two of the most common, kind of like alcohol and marijuana in the drug/alcohol world.

Unhealthy distractions can truly be anything that keeps us from doing what we should be doing or simply broadening ourselves. Gambling. Shopaholic. Porn. Pick one...

I wrote in my first book about how skateboarding can be a drug when done to the point of excluding most everything else in life. There is something very addicting about the slide and glide sports like skateboarding, snow or water skiing, surfing, snowboarding, and so on. As a former water ski junkie who would skip work to catch a sundown or sunup ski on glass-like water, I know how real life seems to pale to the rush we get from such activities. A common bumper sticker and mentality in my current ski resort home of Lake Tahoe is *Real Skiers Don't Have Real Jobs*. They need to be able to easily call in sick on fresh powder days.

I've also been talking about adults the past few years to make a point that distraction is not just a teen thing. I believe that most adults use distraction as just that: a break from the grind and monotony of everyday life and work. Teens, however, who have become more and more irresponsible in the past hundred years or so, have a tendency to distract from life itself. Each year of my career I see more and more teens withdrawing from life, their curiosity squelched by too much distraction and too many adults who model less than desirous behavior, leading teens to not want to join the "grownup" club and end up boring as they perceive many of us adults.

Personally, I feel distractions are becoming more and more prevalent in our fast-moving society. During a recent trip to do some teen consulting in New York, I spent too much time in airports and on planes, and pondered how travel had changed. Twenty years ago I was more prone to have an interesting conversation with someone crossing my path for a few hours. Sitting in airports, we had little to distract us but our books and curiosity about why everyone else was going where they were going.

Now, most people are plugged into their phones or other MP3 players, or staring into their laptop or tablet screens. People with cell phones kill time or conduct business by calling up people from almost anywhere. Cell phone users with portable headsets continue to confuse me by appearing to be talking to me or someone else, only to be carrying on a phone conversation with someone across the country or back at work. Heck, the airlines have continued to feed our TV distraction by showing television shows on the planes.

These distractions are not inherently bad. Like any other addiction, it is about severity and a matter of degree. With teens, I mostly worry about them losing their curiosity about life. So many kids seem to be checked out on what's going on around them. They may be doing poorly or moderately in school, but still have time for a daily fix of reality TV or skateboarding the steps in front of the library. They spend hours in front of video games exercising their thumbs and little else, ignoring much of life going on around them.

There's an old saying: "You can't want something until you know it exists." I'm old enough to remember the invention of 8-track tape players, the first color TV on the block, VCR's, Pong and Atari, FM radio and a million other techno marvels. But was I sitting around as a kid in the 60's complaining because we didn't have the ability to play tapes in our cars? No, we were happy to sit and listen to the radio and hope to hear our favorite songs. When radio reception evaporated we lapsed into conversations and travel games.

We didn't sit at pizza parlors wishing we had arcade games to play, because the whole concept of arcade games had not been invented yet. I remember having only one TV channel (CBS) when I was a little kid in Reno, Nevada. Reception was based on how well our rabbit-ear antennae were working. If I didn't want to watch *Ed Sullivan* on Sunday night, I didn't channel surf until I found something more palatable. I opened a book or played a game.

You can't want something until you know it exists. How many times have you and I not had a craving for a certain thing, then absolutely had to have it when it was first invented or offered? Historically, things change slowly, but are now changing exponentially faster. For example, how many thousands of years did people survive with bows and arrows, spears and knives. For thousands of years people did fine with what they had, then of course change came along and gave people something new to want: metal weapons, guns, artillery, etc.

It's been said that the world's greatest technological advances have taken place in the last 2000 years. In those 2000 years, the majority of advancements came in the past 200 years. In those recent 200 years, the biggest changes came in the past 20 years. Of the last 20 years, most change and advancement has come in the past two years, and so on.

On a shorter scale, for much of the 20th century most Americans were happy with radio, then record albums, then TV. We've now learned the pattern of wanting things we don't have: we now know there must be something better and more distracting than we just had, because that is now the way we experience things. New inventions don't amaze us so much anymore as entice us to get them ASAP. Rather than be content that CD's were more convenient than LP's, we immediately set to replacing them with DVD's which have now also become less popular due to massive hard drive storage and streaming media like Netflix, iTunes, Amazon, and Hulu.

Our teens and other children are caught up in this never-ending spiral to distract ourselves. Contrary to our childhoods, modern teens know a new and better distraction is coming. Heck, that has been the way of their short lives. Modern teens are prisoners to the pattern of planned obsolescence and progress for the sake of progress. They know the next generation of distraction is already on the drawing boards. Now, if they can just keep themselves distracted until it arrives......

Bret Stephenson

Four

The Illusion of Control

I think we are all insecure, and there is nothing wrong in
accepting that. But the problem arises when we try to counter
this insecurity by cultivating this illusion of control, and we
start taking ourselves and everything we know too seriously.
Sushant Singh Rajput

Most of the books about teens I've come across in my career
are largely about behavior management, the politically
correct term for behavior modification. For years I plowed
through books with titles like *Back in Control, Controlling Your
Teen, Teen Shaping* and so on. While most of the material
within these books is applicable to many teens, most fail to
touch on the big question: Why do we need such books? A
hundred years ago we had no need for them.

Since America leads the world in teen violence, teen crime,
teen drug use, and therefore, teen incarceration, the issue does
seem to be about controlling their behavior. I'm most
interested in working on the Cause of teen problems rather
than dealing constantly with their Symptoms: the behavior
we all see. Recall when I was trying to publish my first book
on teen boys, countless agents and publishers lamented my
material was not a "parenting book." Why, I asked, do we

need one more behavior control book when most apparently are not working? Would one more book on

how to get your kid home by curfew or leveraging them into doing the dishes really matter?

I always wonder about the self-help sections of bookstores that offer dozens of titles on one subject. If it is supposedly so clear, why do we need so many books telling us the same thing? I've come to believe that for most American adults and parents, they don't want to work with their teens, but simply control them. This has led to the birth and growth of boot camps, for example, a ludicrous invention to try and beat adolescence out of a teen.

Adolescence is a process and can't be circumvented or minimized. It's like breaking a horse: you can jump on the horse's back and literally run him into the ground, largely breaking his spirit but getting him to obey your commands, or you can take more time and work with the horse, coming to a mutual understanding that benefits both horse and rider. Too many teen programs and models are about breaking the adolescent spirit with control.

First of all, we have to understand how behavior management works. There are essentially three ways to change someone's behavior:

1. Positive reinforcement,
2. Negative consequences or Punishment
3. Neutral reinforcement—No Rewards (kiss me or kick me, but don't ignore me).

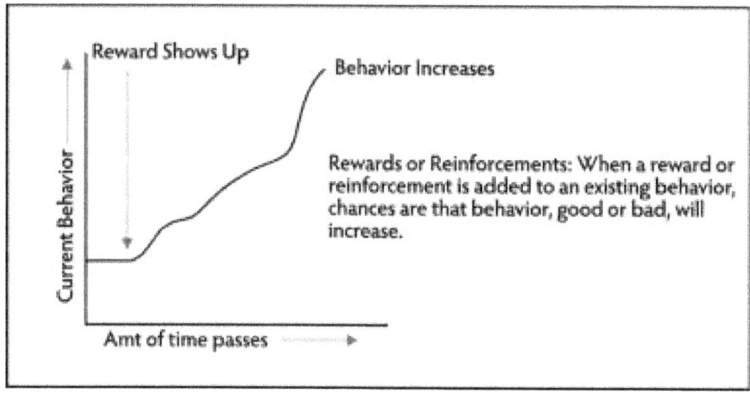

Figure 1--Positive Reinforcement

Positive reinforcement (Figure 1) is getting a reward right after doing the behavior at hand, and is the best way to get what you want. This manifests in real life as a paycheck after weeks of work, or that new mountain bike after saving so hard.

Negative reinforcements (Figure 2) are negative consequences, like getting grounded or having your Nintendo taken away. Punishment is the extreme version of this and actually fails as people get used to it.

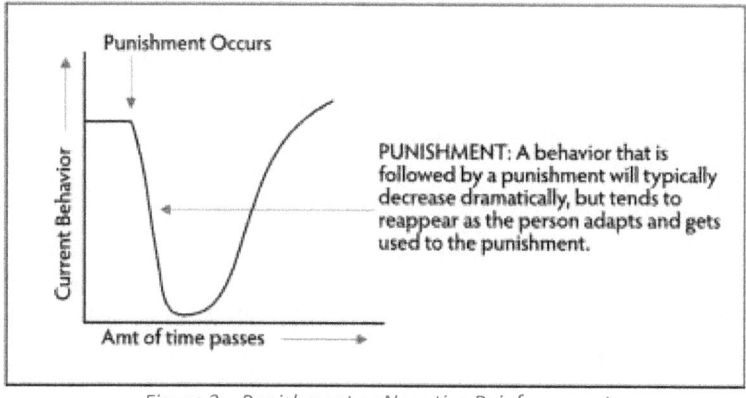

Figure 2—Punishment or Negative Reinforcement

Neutral reinforcement (Figure 3) is getting no reward or real consequence at all, as in ignoring a bully until he needs to go pick on someone else to get his *reward*.

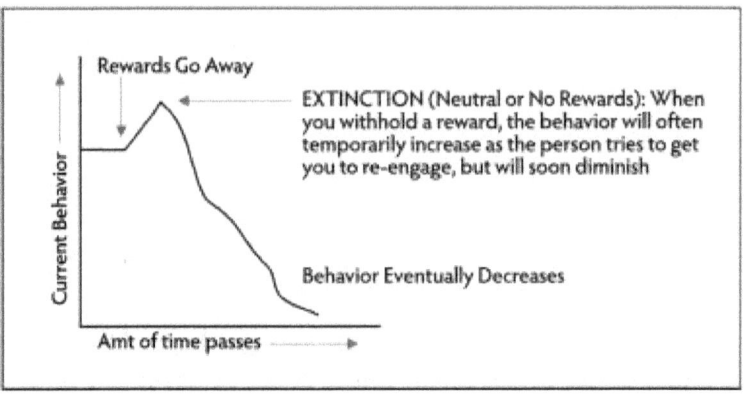

Figure 3--Extinction or Neutral Reinforcement

If the bully receives no reward/reinforcement from you (fear, tears, etc.) he usually moves on to a new target. Most people hate to be ignored, and teens particularly will get attention in a negative way if their positive behavior is overlooked or they don't get any input or feedback at all. No one likes feeling like they don't matter.

Most parenting books about teens focus on the negative aspect: how to give consequences to your teen so he or she will do what you want. However, countless parents have complained to me about how their teen has nothing left to take from their room. All phones, computers, DVD players, Internet access, PlayStations and so on have been pulled but the kid still won't clean his room or get better grades. Heck, many parents have even pulled the bedroom door so their teen cannot hide from the family!

Too often with teens, *it is not about what they are losing for consequences, but what they're not getting as reinforcement*. If you've pulled everything fun from your teen's room and he/she is still acting negatively, it's time to rethink the problem. Ever ponder how they teach a dolphin to jump through a hoop, or get an elephant to stand on a stool? No amount of punishment or negative consequences can leverage the dolphin to swim through a hoop. You simply wait until the dolphin gets close to the hoop, and toss him a tasty morsel as a reward. Any intelligent animal will eventually put two and two together, understanding that if he gets near the hoop he gets a treat. If he touches the hoop, or sniffs around it, for example, he gets three treats. When he finally happens to wander through the hoop: major treats.

The trick with teens is not so much to withhold everything from them but to compromise with helping them get what they want while you get what you want. Thus, instead of stripping their room (especially if it isn't working), ask what they want (more freedom, more allowance, etc.). Then be certain what you want (clean room, better grades, washed dishes, etc.). Make a deal. If he or she will clean their room regularly, you'll up their allowance. If the dishes are done on time, they get a later curfew. No performance, no reward. The trick is to find out what they really want, and that is your leverage, not what they can live without. The trick with teens is not to relentlessly keep saying "No" to them in an effort to control them, but to lead them in a direction that allows you to say "Yes" as often as possible while maintaining family boundaries.

We have to *want* teens to make good choices, not just hope or assume they'll screw up so we can tell them how smart we are. Too often with adults and parents, it comes down to this: by keeping teens *Wrong*, that implies we grownups are *Right*. As long as teens are *Bad*, then we must be *Good*. You can of course see this polarized thinking in many other aspects of our lives. I can't tell you how many times some residential center staff came up to me and breathlessly commented "Well, we caught your boy this morning doing...!" Wow.

He's excited because he caught a delinquent boy I'm close with doing something wrong. I guess I'm supposed to be impressed by this and feel shame I put faith in a kid who still makes mistakes. I'd be much more impressed if the staff member came to me with news of something *good* he caught "my boy" doing.

The most asked question I've had from parents in three decades is this: "Why do they do it?" The answer is simple: Because they can! They do it because, on some level, it works for them. Most teens get away with negative behavior because they learn early that the parents' bluff or threat is empty: "This is your last warning!" What happened after the first warning? Or, "I won't tell you again!" Same issue: what were the consequences for not following the directives the first time? Kids learn early that when mom says No, for example, that means Maybe if you persist long enough.

One of my favorite teen cartoons has two boys talking on a playground. One boy says to the other, "Hey, isn't that your mom calling you to come home?"

"Yeah," says the second boy, "but it's only the second call."

This last paragraph sounds like the kid needs some of that behavioral control I said to be careful about. But let's look at the situation again. Each time a teen gets away with stalling, or doing a poor job at something, they are in essence being rewarded by the lack of consequences. This is the flaw to a lecture as a consequence is there is no real teeth in it. If you say 10 pm is curfew, then your daughter comes in at 10:15 and you just roll your eyes, your 10 pm boundary has been stretched to 10:15, a grace period that will haunt you for years to come. Do you really give consequences for being fifteen minutes late? Absolutely, or the precedent is set. But they do not have to be brutal consequences, but perhaps coming in or leaving 15 minutes early tomorrow or something similar would be fair.

Countless teens have told me their favorite consequence is a parental/adult lecture, because it has no real teeth to it or something they have to give up, except the time used up during the lecture. They let their minds drift to nicer images like the Bahamas for 10 minutes or so while the parents are ranting away, and nod or say "I know" every few minutes so we think they're paying attention. On the contrary, the consequence teens have told me they hate most is closely related: the lecture about when we were their age! While we need to use our own life experiences to give teens a bigger perspective, we can't take it personal when they have trouble relating our adolescent years in another time, place and circumstances to what they are going through right now.

Look at it this way: your daughter goes out and you say be home by 10 pm. To encourage positive behavior, tell her that if she's in the house by 9:59, she can have Reward A (sleepover, movie choice, etc.). If she's home at 10:01, a mere 2-minute swing, she comes in at 9 pm for the next two nights. Which would you choose? Yep, you and the dolphin would take being home early! This is wanting her to succeed. This is hoping she'll make a good choice, not just hoping she'll do what she's supposed to and getting in trouble if she doesn't. See how subtle the difference is?

Finally, logical consequences are the best if you do have to take something away. If your son is abusing phone privileges, take away or limit his phone "reinforcement." If your daughter is pushing curfew, take away free time. And remove the word "punishment" from your vocabulary. Substitute the term "consequence." Punishment is just that; punitive and most often driven by anger or emotions. Consequences are logical ramifications from the behavior.

How can you tell the difference? A punishment cannot be returned and a consequence can, so to speak.

For example, if your daughter comes home an hour late with some 'lame' excuse about a flat tire and you call her a liar (or worse), and later you find out she and her boyfriend really did have a flat tire, can you retract the sting of that name-calling? Nope, the damage is done. But if you kept her home the next night as a logical consequence, and then found out she was actually telling the truth (don't you hate it when teens are right?), could you give back that lost time? Yes, in a couple of ways. You could give her an extra hour here and there, or a Get Out of Jail free card for the next time she is late (there's almost always another next time with teens). Never loft out a threat or bluff you will not, or cannot enforce. Remember, they do it because it rewards them in some fashion. We just have to figure out what their rewards and desires are.

Five

The Adolescent Essence

Essence: something that is, or exists...
　　In every adult ever invented resides
A former tenant, a remnant of growth, an adolescent.

The essence of adolescence is a flavor,
　　Delicious to some yet distasteful to others;
Most often with a dash of both.

Yesterday's youth had a different flavor, an ancient
　　Recipe repeated and refined through generations.
Today is fast food, the art of adolescence supplanted by
　　convenience.

Before, the essence was subtle and special, a taste
　　You could sense but not name. Now the
Flavor is harsh, typical, the same everywhere.

If adolescence had been an animal, it would
　　Have been the cocoon, halfway between
Crawling and flying.

Today's adolescence is a chameleon, wearing masks of
camouflage
　To prevent us looking closely. Or a porcupine, armored
　on the outside
While trying to protect the vulnerable parts underneath.

Where once the transportation of adolescence was
　Courage, today movement is encumbered
By wishful thinking.

Were adolescence to be a business, we would have found
　La Botanica Majica, peddling the magic of life.
Today's version could be part of any strip mall.

If adolescence were a time of day, it would have been
　Midnight, the cusp. Today, adolescence
Is tomorrow, anything but today.

Were adolescence a sound or noise,
　It would once have been a question. Today it
Is a shout, and a whisper.

Should adolescence become something around the house,
　It would have appeared a doorway or passage,
Rather than today's closed door.

Looking back at adolescence as a place,
　We see it was a crossroads,
Now more of a street corner.

The machine of adolescence was paradox, a glue
　Complicated yet simple, only to now be
Anything new and easy, and easily cast aside.

Looked at as a character from another time,
  Adolescence was the Hero, a bigger person waiting to be
  born.
Now, it is James Dean, lonely in isolation, angered by
neglect.

The treasure of adolescence was its metamorphosis, the
  Simple Labyrinth path into adulthood. Today's treasure
Is a silver maze, tarnished and dull from lack of care.

© 2004 Bret Stephenson

I use a wonderful exercise called *Essences* with teens, which was developed by teen guru David Oldfield. Part of a much larger overall scheme, *Essences* is a list of about ten questions designed to help teens abstract a bit out of black and white thinking. But it is also a subtle way to get them to try and tell you more of their essence as a person and young adult. In particular, it attempts to help them look at themselves in a metaphorical way, which gives us youth workers much more interesting material to use with them than plain therapy.

Essences questions include:

- *If you were a time of day, what would that be?* (Teens are very often midnight--dark and light, the magical hour, etc.)
- *If you were something found around the house, what would you be?* (I once had a boy say he felt like an answering machine. The youngest in his family, they seemed to want info from him but were too busy to engage with him or take him very seriously. When not asking him where someone was, he felt

like and unused answering machine.)

- *If you were a place, what would that be?* (One girl once said she felt like a huge mall, except it was empty. She felt like it was a place she was supposed to be at her age, but she felt her mall was empty and looking to her to fill it up.)

A number of years ago I was guiding a group of adult participants through one of my Hero's Journey workshops. I was having them fill out Essences. While I was waiting, I got the idea to try and answer the Essences question from an archetypal perspective, as if I was answering for all adolescents and not just my own journey. The poem above was my sense of how the overall adolescent essence is.

David Oldfield's wonderful curriculum *The Journey* can be found at www.midwaycenter.com.

Six

From Irresponsibility to Responsibility

Adolescence is society's permission slip for combining physical
maturity with psychological irresponsibility.
Terri Apter

From a developmental perspective, adolescence is the shifting from the dependency of childhood to the independence of adulthood, or from the irresponsibility of childhood to the responsibility of adulthood. In its deepest sense, adolescence is the process of going from boyhood or girlhood to manhood and womanhood, deeper and fuller aspects of self than mere adulthood.

One of the major mistakes made in modern culture over the past century is letting go of the challenge-based processes that created healthy Men and Women by creating an age-arbitrary system where adult rewards are bestowed on the youth of a culture based on age versus the original worthiness model. This creates modern legal Adults, but doesn't guarantee they are Men or Women. For the vast majority of human history, regardless of whether you're a creationist or evolutionist, teens have been in the thick of day-to-day survival and family or community business.

Allow your mind to wander over all your experiences with not only other cultures, but even America from the early 1900's on back. Remember movies, books, museums, your own travel, and other input you've received on how life was run before what we commonly call modern times. Can you imagine anywhere 80-100 years ago where all that was expected of a teenager was to sit around doing the equivalent of playing Nintendo or hanging out idly at a mall? Probably not, because until the early 1900's most teens were deep in the details of everyday survival with their families.

Once adolescents were big enough, they helped with farm duties, or perhaps the family business if the family had moved into the city. Or they held many of the menial jobs such as grocery deliveries, cleaning people or stockroom clerks, giving most if not all of their wages back to the family. Everyone was busy: even little children to the extent they could help the family survive. Teens simply could not have been allowed to just "kick it" or "chill out."

This is where some folks will bring up child labor laws, which actually came about to prevent smaller children from being overworked and underpaid in sweat shops, if not treated miserably. But teens can often handle the strain of adult work, particularly the older teens. Where we went wrong was in taking this responsibility away from them, slowly but surely, and expecting them to mostly attend school.

I believe, so to speak, that America came out of World War II more white-collar than the more blue-collared folks who entered WWII. The new Nuclear Family model, atomic energy, computers, GI Bill, TV, jets and overall new predisposition to machines meant that teens had even less to do and hence next came the after-school, extracurricular activities. The most criminal thing we have done after taking their responsibility away is in holding this propensity for irresponsibility against teenagers in general.

I believe teens should work, if possible, as it helps build character and yes, responsibility. Many programs geared toward emancipating teens or giving them independent living skills continue to be delivered in a classroom format. We often don't have viable vocational training or apprenticeships in real settings. We expect all kids to go to college although the majority do not. If only about 30% of Americans have a college degree, then there is a 70% failure rate on the college-track model.

Locally, I've been involved with projects that taught kids woodworking, building web pages, selling custom design clothing and other items, and teaching them culinary arts. Other programs like Homeboy Industries in East L.A. have taken gang kids and put them to work in their own merchandising project using the fascinating slogan: *Nothing Stops a Bullet Like a Job.*

Believe me, most teens want to work. It feeds into their goal to become independent and autonomous, and makes them feel like part of the adult community. In summer 2014, it was estimated that only one third of all teens could find summer employment in the US, and only 25% of teens can find work during the school year. I've been trying to launch youth employment and entrepreneurial models for a number of years now, to teach teens what life in the real world is like rather than trying to tell them in a classroom. I can envision a number of models where not only do the youth work, but run the web site, manage the inventory, learn bookkeeping and distribution, and sell the product or service directly. Each group or clique of kids can contribute as this model encourages youth from all backgrounds and skills to participate.

I've run into many people who supported this concept and just as many who believe teens are inherently broken and will destroy or corrupt anything they touch. We're wary when they hang out on street corners, but we refuse to provide a teen center for them to visit, then complain because they stare at a computer screen or video game all day, or we adults build malls to attract them into shallow spending.

I don't have problems finding teens who want to work. Many teens who will gravitate to trade work are not content to work retail or indoor jobs. In summer 2005 I tried to launch a local landscaping project for youth who didn't want to work at McDonalds or retail stores. Lake Tahoe, a huge alpine lake in California and Nevada, had a new environmental criterion that created an abundance of work, largely manual labor. The project didn't get off the ground, but not because I couldn't get teens interested. I couldn't find adults who felt teens would do as good a job as adults, or that they'd cause too many problems, or be flaky.

When it came to calling me back or following through, the teens were far more responsible than the adults because it was work they were interested in. Another problem with this effort was related to the concept from a century ago that teen labor takes away adult jobs and will work for lower wages. However, in this environmental project there were literally thousands of sites to bring up to the new codes and with an average cost of $3500, most families ignored the mandate trusting that thousands of homeowners would not be fined en masse. Our cost using teen labor averaged $1500-$2000, a benefit to homeowners and the environmental criteria trying to get implemented.

Thus, rather than support a less expensive model for homeowners and give many teens some real life work experience, the project was ignored and unsupported by many adults. So the contractors are still not getting the higher adult wages they were worried about since they aren't being hired anyway. In addition, the lake is not getting any cleaner and the teens are still looking to be productive. No one wins where everyone could have.

For teens, if things do not interest them directly, they often ignore them. When they are invested in the topic or process, they will often surprise us with their enthusiasm and work ethic.

We keep making models and building programs that expect teens to fit the model, rather than making the model fit the teens. Too many adults are guilty of remembering how it was when they were kids, and thinking that modern teens face only the same trials and obstacles as we did. Times have changed, and we need to work on getting teens to be more responsible. The responsibility for that, however, lies with us adults.

Seven

Cause and Effect in the Teen World

According to the Law of Cause and Effect, every effect must have a cause. In other words, everything that happens has a catalyst; everything that came into being has something that caused it. Things don't just happen by themselves.
Ray Comfort

Teen behavior, weird as it may seem, usually has some sort of reasoning behind it. Even the classic 'shock factor' approach of a kid saying, for example, "I don't believe in God," has the goal of seeing how the parents or adults present will act. Similarly, out-of-control behavior does not just pop up unannounced without some progression from small infractions to larger ones, even criminal ones. Often, we adults sit back and watch teens get out of control with few or inefficient consequences for those actions. We tend to intervene too late in the process, putting more emphasis and money into Treatment vs. Prevention

The world of adolescence is governed by the laws of Cause and Effect, as is the rest of the universe. Like anyone else in denial, teens have a magical form of thinking that seems, they hope, to make them immune to this most basic of physics laws. Most younger children easily subscribe to the laws of Cause and Effect, often only on faith from a trusted loved one or caregiver. For instance, when we tell our younger kids that the stove burner is hot, more often than not they will believe us and not tempt fate by testing it.

However, the process of adolescence compels teens, particularly boys, to touch the burner, to find out if the abstract truth we told them earlier is true in their new adolescent reality. This most basic of adolescent laws is where so many adults go wrong in dealing with teens. Most young kids believe the bulk of what their parents tell them about the adult world. This is an abstract situation in that we are telling them that what they learn *now* will possibly benefit them in the *future*, kind of like what they told us about algebra or chemistry. If you're one of those people who have not had to use your rusty algebra skills as an adult, then the abstract truth your teachers told you has not manifested in the truth of reality. The biggest dilemma in this concept is when we tell our children that if they do X, then Y will happen—and then it doesn't happen.

Heck, just a year or two ago we were contentedly watching Harry Potter and Shreck with our sweet kids. They believed faithfully in our description of what happens when you tamper with the laws of the land--if X then Y: steal and go to jail, lie and you'll get caught, skip school and you'll ruin your adult life. The breakdown happens when we adults do not back up the bluffs and threats we've issued previously.

Almost any parent can tell you what happens when you tell a child X will happen if they don't perform a certain task and we neglect to follow through on the Effect, or consequence: we've set a dangerous precedent for the next time, and our boundaries are stretched. If you've ever found yourself saying "This is your last warning!" or "How many times have I asked you to..." then you know the feeling. The big question is what initially happened as an Effect or consequence after the first warning? Something inefficient or even missing.

First, we seem to take it personal that the teen doesn't believe us about the burner. We grownups really need to understand that it is not only normal for teens to test the burner, but that they need to do so in order to grow. Most of us adults know we learn our best lessons in life from our mistakes and trials. We know, hard as it is, that we have to let our small child fall off his or her bike once or twice in order to learn the reality of how to ride a bike and what happens if you do not pay attention on one. The process of adolescence often requires that the teen, or pre-teen, test the abstract concept by testing it in reality. This is why it is so critical for ALL adults to hold their boundaries with teens: to be the reality we warned them about so long ago. Our actions must be congruent with what we actually say and do.

Second, teens absolutely hate it when adults say or model "Do what I say, not what I do." Teens are the masters at finding hypocrisy and double standards in the adult world. Why? Because they are looking for loopholes to all that reality we told them about earlier in life. Wouldn't it be nice, they think, if all those bad things the adults told us would happen didn't manifest after all?? This makes the abstract messages of reality they received as children worthless.

Then, teens carry it a step further. If X apparently wasn't true, then maybe A, B or C won't be. This creates a pattern or model for them to challenge everything for that hopeful loophole. If you haven't read between the lines yet, this means we grownups have to model what we say very accurately. It has been this growing chasm of what we say versus what we do that has teens testing and challenging more and more each generation. They're trying to confirm where the reality is we told them about. As we change our values and norms in society, so do teens, and not always in the most elegant way. But scores of cultures have helped their teens adapt without all drama we have in modern times.

I worked with a 16-year-old boy once who had been arrested for selling crack cocaine nine times, and had just been sent to his first treatment center. Of course his behavior was inappropriate and he deserved his consequences, but I had to ask, what happened with the first eight arrests to remind him of the reality we told him about as a kid when we explained what happens when a person breaks the law? He'd received a few hand-slaps in the guise of probation violations, failed drug tests, a few nights here and there in juvenile detention and so on, but nothing to really sway him from selling more. So following the laws of Cause and Effect, or Cause and Symptoms, whose fault is this rebellious behavior really attributed to? Teens, because they are built to take the path of least resistance if possible, or us grownups for telling them one thing and then letting them walk down a different path than we told them about? This is a good example of positive reinforcement for a negative behavior.

On a larger note, we have to ask ourselves if the growing incidents of teen anger, decline in school performance, violence, drug use, gangs, and so on are Caused by the teen culture, or if they are more accurately the Effect or symptom of larger societal problems affecting them. Teens are deeply impacted by the adult values and behavior around them, and can mostly just react to those dynamics as most are out of their control. So while it is easy to blame teens for many of our problems in our communities, my experience is that teens are telling us how they feel with their behavior, and too often we don't listen enough to make necessary or occasional changes. They are not always wrong in their insatiable idealism and feelings for the way things *should* be.

Eight

Cultural Mirrors

We only see what we want to see; we only hear what we want to hear. Our belief system is just like a mirror that only shows us what we believe.
Don Miguel Ruiz

One of the great undervalued services teens perform for us is acting as a cultural mirror for society. They reflect back to us the world as they see and feel it. Basically, our role as adults and parents is to listen, to respond when necessary, change what should be changed, and explain why some things they don't like simply are that way and they need to accept that.

As mentioned elsewhere in this book, the end of adolescence can be described as the shift in thinking from the way things *should be* to accepting the way *things are*. We're all aware of the angst teens often get in not liking the situation around them. We parents are often referred to as lame, old fashioned, close-minded and so on. Too often we either don't truly hear our teens' complaints, or dismiss them without much thought. We forget how much has changed for teens since we were their age. I figure we adults can resonate with about 50% of what teens are experiencing nowadays. We were all 13, 15 and 17, but not in this day and age.

But part of the adolescent process, similar to rebelling and testing, is to tell us the outcome or feelings when they run into something that doesn't fit their expectations. They reflect back to us their discontent and it is short-sighted of us to dismiss what they say out of hand without reflecting on it. Values and beliefs change from generation to generation and teens are constantly having to adapt to the adult word around them. Often, teens see or perceive a change in societal shifts before we adults do. Some obviously do this more gracefully than others.

Like any other reflection, sometimes we look in the mirror and are not especially happy with what we see there. This is often the case with teens who make us look at ourselves and our paths. Many people project their own fears and discontent back on the teens because it's easier to blame them than change ourselves. In a way, we often make teens *wrong* so we are inherently *right*. Or we make them *bad* so we are essentially *good*. The trick here is to accept the reflection as something to review and ponder.

Most parents want to help their children and teens avoid 'unnecessary' situations or problems. However, often when we look at teens we see our own younger behavior and want to stop current youth from following in our footsteps or making the same mistakes we did. We are forced to review the pre-marital sex we had, often unprotected. We see the current teen drug and alcohol experimentation through the lenses of what we did, or maybe kids heading into stealing or other delinquent behavior we may have experience with. Parents run into this dilemma all the time when issues of sex, drugs, school, and other behaviors pop up when our kids hit adolescence. We have to find a way with integrity to offer up our experiences and history without preaching or pretending we never did any of the things currently inhabiting your teen's life.

Teens often comment to me their thoughts and fears about global terrorism, nuclear war, changes in the climate and environment, corrupt politicians, corporate criminals, inner-city conditions, poverty, the lack of good jobs, high cost of education and so on. Teens may not be *right* in their descriptions or facts, but that does not invalidate their feelings and fears. If we fail to engage in these conversations with our teens then we are essentially telling them we are uninterested and unwilling to help. That, of course, leads to a breakdown in communication with teens, that is often irretrievable once broken.

When we look at our reflections in a mirror and don't like what we see, then we know we have to change things in our life to look and/or feel better. When teens reflect back to us, we often fail to realize they may be right or have a good point we should entertain. Teens serve a great purpose for society in this process, constantly testing and challenging the adult world to see what is true, real, necessary, and so on. If we don't do this, we might as well blame our own literal mirror reflection for our behavior of being overweight, too gray, or whatever we literally see.

When teens reflect back to us aspects of their lives, it is really unthinkable not to engage with them. We need to be strong and honest enough to look back at them and tell them what we know and what we don't know without judgment. They will not ignore a fun behavior just because you may have had a negative experience with it. Being adolescents, they will have to test things anyway, so we might as well help them walk as stable a path through the teen years as possible.

Nine

Boundaries are like a Boxing Ring

*Adolescents are not monsters. They are just people trying to
learn how to make it among the adults in the world,
who are probably not so sure themselves.*
Virginia Satir

The boundaries we use to try and guide teens (and younger kids as well) should be like the ropes in a boxing ring: tight and firm but somewhat flexible. We parents and adults spend a lot of time telling our children as they are growing up what behavior is expected of them, and what consequences will happen to them if they break the family's or society's rules and boundaries.

By boundaries I mean what the family's rules are regarding curfew, grades, dating, drugs, school and so on. Adolescence was designed for teens to test these boundaries to see if what we told them will happen will really happen or not. That's kind of a simplistic explanation but overall very accurate. We all know what happens when you suggest, or tell, a defiant teen not to do something—they usually do it to see what happens. This s mostly true of boys, but certainly not all the tie. Also, many teens are drawn to the taboo of "no" to see what all the fuss is about.

The ropes in a boxing ring are literal, physical boundaries to keep the fighters in a designated area. If the ring was too large, one of the boxers would simply be able to avoid the more aggressive or stronger boxer altogether. If the ropes, or boundaries were too close then you'd have a slugfest where neither fighter could get any space or rest from the other. So overall you need a space large enough to move around within while not being too big to be useful. Professional boxers argue for ring size in their negotiations to get a ring size that suits their style. An old school slugger wants a small ring so his opponent cannot get far away. Conversely, boxers who move a lot like Muhammed Ali, want all the room they can get.

The same dynamics apply with you and your teens. You need to have common, average boundaries with your teens, like a normal sized boxing ring. Much adult frustration comes when, after we adults set up our perfect boundaries of say, five meters, our teens push against them again and again. This is the process of adolescence, and our job as parents and adults is to push the boundaries back to the original size.

Pretend your boundaries are similar to a 16-foot boxing ring. Let's say the curfew for your daughter is 10 pm. If she comes in at 10:15 and you don't really do anything about it, your 10 pm boundary now has an implied 15-minute grace period and the precedent has been set. In essence, your boundaries are now at 16 feet and 6 inches, so to speak. If you enact appropriate consequences that make your daughter not want to test your boundaries again, then you have reset your boundaries back to the original 16 feet level. Let her get away with her curfew violation and you are no longer at the desired 15 feet.

After some hard effort by you to reestablish your curfew boundaries, next she may push phone boundaries, or dating, perhaps letting her grades drop or cutting a class. Each one of these tests is an attempt to stretch your boundaries from the original 16-foot level, for your teen to try and achieve 17,

18, even 20+ foot boundaries where they can have more fun and less responsibility.

When parents contact me to help get their kids back in control, I often find that over a period of time the family boundaries have been stretched way out because effective consequences were not enforced. In hindsight, it was a small test here, and a small boundary-pushing there. Sixteen feet became 17, not too bad at the time. Seventeen feet then became 18, then 20 and so on. It doesn't take long for kids to become out of control like this. Often, by the time I am brought into the situation, we can't even find the boundaries as they've been stretched so far. The parents' boundaries have been trampled to the ground like an old fence.

Once a mother came to see me, complaining about her son running away. When I asked mother when he ran away, she looked at me quizzically for a moment, then said, "Which time?" Come to find out, this was the third time he had run away from home. My next question was what happened the first two times to dissuade him from running again. Her answer, and attempt at consequences, was weak and her son knew this. He was more willing to play hard ball then she was. And for a really good time, like a rave or other concert, many teens will easily absorb a minor consequence with no real impact.

The best functioning teens I know come from parents who are slightly to the strict side of things. Their boundaries are firm; the teens know the boundaries and usually what will happen if they test the boundaries. The teens and families with the most behavior problems come from parents who don't enforce family boundaries and the kids slowly slide into out-of-control behavior with questionable boundaries. Many people assume most of my out-of-control kids are all from inner-city poverty situations with classically dysfunctional parents, but I'm seeing more and more spoiled kids getting out of control. Heck, Hollywood makes plenty of movies describing the antics of entitled well-to-do youth acting out.

Remember, teens do not become out-of-control overnight. They just don't run away for three days without a progression of increasingly negative behavior leading up to it. When parents tell me their teen is out-of-control, that he has run away three times in the past few weeks, I know there have been a long series of broken boundaries without effective consequences to sway the teen from doing so again.

In essence, your boxing ring boundaries are three dimensional. Your son or daughter will push the north-south boundaries, and about the time you get that straightened out they then push the east-west ones. They can also push up-down, so to speak, because they are very adept at finding loopholes with strange justifications and rationalizations for their behavior. We adults need to be aware of which way our teens are pushing our boundaries and react accordingly.

Getting kids back in control is not easy, and progressively harder the more out-of-control they have become. Like gaining and losing weight, it is far easier and quicker to put on 20 pounds than it is to lose those same 20 pounds. I'm beginning to mix my metaphors, so I'd better move on. With issues like curfew, grades, dating, alcohol, driving and so on, make sure your teen knows what the consequences will be, and follow through with those consequences. Plan for things in these areas to possibly go wrong, so when they do you keep your head and don't have to react emotionally on the spot.

Keep your boundaries tight. Your kids will thank you for it later on in life. We have to play the long game.

Ten

Adolescence is a Baseball Game

To an adolescent, there is nothing in the world more
embarrassing than a parent.
Dave Barry

The process of adolescence is like a baseball game in a couple of ways. First, you have to have two teams to have a game with both an offensive team and a defensive one. This symbiotic struggle is one of the most misunderstood aspects of adolescence. Teens typically assume the offensive role, which is why we parents often feel defensive around our teens.

Teens have to have boundaries. Why? As we discussed in the previous chapter, so they can test them to see if they're real, if the consequences we warned them about will really happen or not. Too many adults seem to believe that teens should believe everything we adults tell them. In a way that is logical and makes sense, but ask yourself this: did you do everything the adults in your teen world told you or did you try and get away with some negative stuff? Did that make you bad or defiant, or just a curious teenager?

Also, kids are very adept at seeing the difference between what many of us say and do. As small children we may likely buy into "Do as I say and not as I do" but as teens they see through this double standard and wonder about possible loopholes in what we taught them. If they start to find discrepancies, particularly within their family, they can begin to wonder what other do's and don'ts we've told them may not hold up to testing or scrutiny

In modern times we often have issues with the mere fact that our teen is challenging us, like it is a personal affront of some kind. We spend our kids' childhoods telling them the bad things that will happen if they misbehave: steal a car and go to juvenile detention, cut school and get suspended, break curfew and get grounded. But in the game of adolescence they often have to test these potential realities, to see if the abstract lectures they have heard repeatedly will manifest into everyday life.

It is this proof, the experiencing of logical consequences for one's actions, that is infinitely a better teacher than a continuing lecture of what *might* happen. Kids do not test every aspect, at least initially. What they learn from a handful of attempts is what will usually encourage them to make their own decisions about all the other possible tests. This is why it is critical to not let your children get away with breaking rules and boundaries, particularly early in adolescence.

So for this process, or cycle to complete itself, we need two teams in our symbolic baseball game: adults and teens. If we simply shut down the teens and their testing because we may be more experienced, stronger, or faster, we don't have a game but a forfeit of one strong team only. This is what many boot camp programs try to do: squelch adolescence entirely by breaking the adolescent spirit.

This is why teens need to have a team to play against. Here's how it works, or should work. As the adult in the game, imagine you are the pitcher on defense. Your son or daughter is a runner on first base. Your goal is to keep your teen from stealing second base. You may be very good at this and have a handful of tricks and skills you can use. You could literally try to pick him or her off. Or you could try a pitch-out with your catcher. You can step off the mound to change up your timing.

Basically, you use all of your wiles, skills and tricks to keep this player from stealing second base. Now, reverse the roles. As a (teen) player on first base, their goal is to get to second base. They also have some tricks up their sleeve, such as faking a run and jerking around to distract you. Your teen has an opposing goal to your own. Your job is to stop the steal—their job is to complete the steal.

For this adolescent life-game to complete itself the pitcher (adult) needs to stop the runner most of the time. But the teen needs to steal second base successfully some of the time too. You may not like them getting to second base in this figurative game, but if they don't get some sort of success there, they will look elsewhere we can't control the game so much.

The overall game ends after a number of tedious years in a tie. Why a tie? *Conflicting needs.* Because guiding teens through adolescence is not about beating them or winning which creates losers, but helping them become better players in life so they can start early adulthood with a feeling of growth. And the teen cannot 'win' because that gives them too much power over adults during the teen years. So it is frustrating, but best, to essentially play to a tie, until they outgrow the game and move into more mature adult thinking and the game ends. Essentially, you have a game that goes back and forth for years, only to have the teen team stop competing one day. Then you can rest!

Many adults at this point complain that this process should not be a game, that the adults should determine the outcome and avoid any competition from young people. Almost 30 years with teens has led me to disagree. Respect for elders is not a rule, but a value learned and earned. Simply beat teens into submission and you'll win the battle but lose the longer war. I've stated that teens need boundaries to test. The other reality I've learned is that most teens <u>will</u> test their boundaries to some degree, so hoping they won't is overly idealistic. Some teens obviously test harder than others. Teens also need to learn to keep in perspective how short adolescence is in the scope of a human life.

Kids that are out of control are usually kids who tested boundaries early and got away with it, so they push harder and each unchecked boundary becomes the new precedent or baseline of behavior. There was no parental pitcher to help hone their skills and abilities, so they develop an entitlement or magical thinking that they can get away with almost anything because it worked before. Having soft family or personal boundaries is like giving your teen too much of a lead on first base--they'll get a better chance to reach second base successfully and you'll be frustrated because they did.

Since most teens <u>are</u> going to test boundaries, then what smart adults will do is prepare as much as possible. Work with the adolescent process and you stand a good chance of a positive outcome. Try to fight the adolescent spirit and you'll find it one of the most stubborn things ever invented. Thus, you must become the best pitcher you can, by playing firm but fair.

Thus, this metaphorical baseball game must play to a tie of sorts, a 237 inning game with no real winner or loser. You match your teen tit for tat. They push a boundary, and you put it back. They test a rule; you enforce it so they know it is real. What you have warned them will happen if they misbehave has happened. One day, somewhere near the end of adolescence (around 18 give or take) they will usually quit the game. Why? Because they are finally ready to join the "big leagues," the world of adults, and the game will continue when they have children. Their thinking shifts away from the way things "should be" to the way things are. If they slide through this critical learning period without this process, you'll find adult adolescent behavior in grownups who keep trying to beat the System the easy way.

Eleven

Whetstones of Life

*Give me six hours to chop down a tree and I will spend
the first four sharpening the axe.*
Abraham Lincoln

To really sharpen the edge of a knife, it must be honed against something of equal or harder material. After all, you cannot sharpen a knife or other blade on a piece of wood or similar softer material. For our purposes, teens are the knives or blades requiring sharpening. Of course, teens will usually tell us how 'sharp' they think they are and how 'dull' we adults and parents are, but as is often the case, they are mistaken. We adults are the much less glamorous role—the whetstone.

We spend our children's early years helping form them into a useful and functional being. Much like a knife, chisel or other such object, once forged into its basic shape, a fine edge still needs to be added. Being the whetstone or grindstone in life is not the most alluring position, but it is a crucial one or our children remain "dull." The recent trend toward standardization of schools, evidence-based only therapeutic approaches, the failure of the self-esteem movement, and the failure of "programs" not supported by the community have left too many teens unsharpened and ill prepared for the challenges of life.

In 1899 the first juvenile justice court was established in the US. One of the concepts to come out of that period was the adoption of the government of *parens patriae*, which gave the government the ability to act as legal parent and remove children from their homes and families. While this made sense to a degree to remove kids from unhealthy homes, the long-term result was that parents began deferring parental decisions to the schools and governments. For example, with the addition during the Industrial Revolution of *status offenses* written specifically against teens, a 13-year-old boy drinking alcohol or skipping school became a legal matter and not so much a family matter anymore.

Many modern parents have relinquished their sharpening duties to schools and other teen-related aspects. Schools were never meant to parent our kids. Sharpen their minds, sure, but not their overall character and essence. But this is not just a parental problem but a community challenge. The vast majority of human history has been lived in small communities, many or most with initiation and rite of passage practices for sharpening their youth in to healthy adults, men and women.

Many teens are curious about life and will look for people and experiences that will sharpen them. Conversely, many teens inherently try to take the path of least resistance, which may provide a short term gain but fails to sharpen them into stronger and more independent individuals.

Teens have to be taught, hopefully in a creative and positive way, that keeping one's "nose to the grindstone" is the best way to sharpen themselves, build endurance, character and responsibility—all critical aspects for a healthy adulthood.

Twelve

I Think, Therefore I Deserve...

I think; therefore, I am the center of the universe.
Craig Bruce

One of the most frustrating dynamics of adolescence is the feeling of entitlement that many teens have. According to the dictionary the term entitlement means "the right somebody has to do or receive something." This is not inherently a bad thing, for many people deserve or have the right to something, such as a hard-earned vacation.

But for many teens, the concept of entitlement is more about what they feel they are deserving of, or even owed, with little or no effort on their part. Using the vacation example above, they expect a vacation without the hard-earned part. It is as if the universe owes them special or privileged treatment for simply being born. This manifests in unlimited ways, from teens acting as if household chores are beneath them to expecting adults and parents to give them cars, cool technology, large allowances and so on.

My experience with teen entitlement has shown me little difference overall between poorer youth and teens coming from affluent families. On one hand it makes sense that if a child comes from a family without many financial resources and support, he or she will wish that they had more. I recall my own sense of entitlement as a teen. My father did not make much money and I felt so special, so preordained to have better things than he could afford. This feeling of the world owing me more than I had led to my stealing regularly, justifying my actions with the notion that since my father was allegedly unsuccessful and I deserved special things, I was allowed to pursue them in whatever means justified my ends.

Many of the wealthier teens I've worked with also had entitlement, brought on by getting more treats and goods than their peers or friends, or perhaps being told that their affluent status means they get special privileges and consideration. I recall two brothers about 15 years ago, sons of a surgeon, who complained in our counseling sessions that at Christmas, the older boy only got $12,000 worth of video equipment. The younger boy complained of only getting three new snowboards, so he'd have to change his wax too often. Imagine the value of these treats in today's economy, and that these kids felt slighted somehow.

The big question is, whose fault is this behavior and belief system, really? Dad, the surgeon, was ready to put them in a 6-12 month youth behavior camp because he "didn't have time" for teen issues. By my standards, their misbehavior was minimal, with only one real anger outburst reported from the youngest boy once. It was clear that dad simply had no time or patience to give to his boys. So he tried to buy his way out of it with toys and distractions, and when that failed, he blamed the kids for his inattention to parenting and chose to toss away more money in a geographic cure by sending the boys to a treatment facility. Their belief that the world owed them more was already deeply ingrained and without any of his behavior or beliefs changing, neither did theirs.

In recent years, I've witnessed the diagnosis of Conduct Disorder shift from almost exclusively poor, delinquent youth to affluent, overly-spoiled kids who cannot empathize with others. Many Millennials are stereotyped as showing a lack of forward drive and persistence. A couple generations now of the self-esteem concept that everyone should win has failed to build tenacity and endurance in many modern youth. Many current young people have not learned the art of hard work and persistence as they were too often praised for mediocre efforts and outcomes.

Teen entitlement is related to a couple of other adolescent developmental dynamics. It overlaps with the problem that teens often are also egocentric; that they believe the world revolves around them. This is also common with toddlers and preschoolers. When someone is egocentric they feel at the heart of everything, and any changes to their universe are first perceived by how it affects or impacts the teen. Parents' jobs, new car purchases, or decisions to move the household are often run through these "me" filters, with the teen only able to see how any action immediately, if indirectly, affects them.

Entitlement also is related to the fact many teens have difficulty abstracting--handling issues and concepts that are not concrete and are multidimensional. In the black & white, either/or thinking common to many teens, the world *should* be a more amenable place for them. In a perfect world, they would be literally entitled to more cell phones, video games and less schoolwork. This ties in with, and overlaps with the teen propensity for idealism.

Peer pressure, another developmental issue, also feeds into entitlement by having other teens continually remind the boy or girl of what they "should" have or own to be cool and accepted. "On a perfect day", thinks an entitled teen, "I'd have all the cool things I deserve and I'd fit in nicely." The perfect clothes, car, boy/girlfriend, technology, and anything else that helps the teen feel like they have as much or more than everyone else. Of course our American propensity toward consumerism and materialism certainly sets a poor example.

All of these related dynamics reflect a teen's inability to have empathy for those around him. Empathy is the ability to identify with and understand another person's feelings or situation. Thus, if teens are feeling like they're at the center of everything, that the world owes them more, then they are not going to be very empathic with how others feel. This requires being willing and able to see the situation through lenses other than the teen's. Interestingly, teens are so preoccupied with how they think they are being perceived by others, they miss the point that most the other teens are doing the same thing and are focused on themselves as well! Get two egocentric teens in the same room and neither will be paying attention to how the other feels.

In trying to overcome entitlement in a teen, creating empathy is the first place to start, I believe. Building empathy helps a teen see they are not at the center of the universe, that they are not inherently entitled to more than they have, and that the world is often an unfair place where life is seldom black and white, but largely lived in the gray area. But building empathy is not easy with youth who feel the world owes them something. It is often a long and difficult process to plant empathic seeds. Entitlement basically ends if you can get a teen to accept the way the world is versus the way they think it should be.

We adults need to keep an eye and ear out for anything the teen says or does that might imply he or she is amenable to a life lesson regarding empathy for others. Perhaps a movie plot has touched them in some way that you can build from or use as a starting place. Maybe a news article about war or famine in another country will allow you to help them explore feelings about other people.

There have been times when I took something from a teen, "stole" their baseball hat or other important item. This is a risky gesture, obviously, but it has helped an angry teen see how it feels to be a victim, how it feels to lose something in an unfair way. While many teens will get the message when something negative happens to them, many others will internalize yet another unfairness that has happened to them, which in turn reinforces their victimhood.

I love movies for working entitlement issues. Most teens will let down their defenses while watching movies. A careful observer will note a comment or question from a teen that indicates maybe they are pondering how someone in the plot feels, or they note unfairness in the movie you can capitalize on. It was this usefulness of using movies with teens and the adults around them that led to my second book *The Undercurrents of Adolescence: Tracking the Evolution of Modern Adolescence and Delinquency Through Classic Cinema.* For example, in *The Breakfast Club*, Molly Ringwald's spoiled girl character is astounded when after cutting school to go clothes shopping, she actually has to attend detention with the more stereotypical troublemakers.

Often you can have a teen write about how they believe it must feel to be in someone else's shoes, such as being born in Somalia or having a war in your Syrian neighborhood. Remember, many boys in our culture are taught early how not to express their emotions, so boys may have difficulty expressing what they feel, and will more often than not tell you what they think or believe. That's OK, it's a place to start.

The important thing about working a sense of entitlement is not to let it go unchecked. Also, like so many aspects of adolescence, much of our parental or adult success comes in preventing many of these more difficult dynamics from taking root. Talking with your kids early on about what is possible and what is not possible within the family, about the unfair and unpredictable nature of life may help them from feeling entitled.

Getting young children to empathize with others is a key factor to preventing entitlement from taking hold. Teaching children early to work for what they want also helps prevent entitlement by showing them an avenue to get what they want in life. Teaching your kids to give back through service to others is a great prevention tool, like helping feed the homeless a couple times a month. A sure way to create entitlement in children is for parents to speak and act as victims, blame the System or others for all of their personal problems, and so on.

And, as always, we grownups must watch our own idiosyncrasies and personal dynamics in working with teens. We must remain fluid, malleable and willing to work with teens that are less than eager to change, or can't see the reason or necessity to change. Allowing them to float through life feeling entitled will only bring them grief as the world doesn't support their self-demands. The universe can be a good but harsh teacher sometimes, but often teens will allow the entitlement feelings to lead them down a dark road to self-centered and sometimes criminal behavior to get what they "are owed."

Thirteen

The Labyrinth vs the Maze

With a labyrinth, you make a choice to go in - and once
you've chosen, around and around you go. But you always
find your way to the center.
Jeff Bridges

I was in a maze. No matter which way I turned,
it was the wrong way.
Umberto Eco

Adolescents can have an overwhelming drive to shake off all remnants of childhood and discover who they can be. Because this urge to overthrow childhood and embrace something new and exciting can so easily lead teens into trouble, we adults need to be looking out for them and stepping in when they need us to. But we also need to understand that their urge toward growth will not be denied, and we must know how to work with it rather than try to eradicate it.

Initiations and rites of passage were designed to channel these undeniable forces in teens, not neutralize them. Rather than forcing kids to fit an adult concept of the process, older cultures built systems to fit the teens' needs, and therefore ran into much less confrontation and resistance than we currently experience in modern, *civilized* times.

The difference between the traditional, ritual-based approach to the developing adolescent and the modern approach is comparable to the difference between a maze and a labyrinth. A maze is built to be confusing to the participant. Blind alleys and blocked paths confuse and confound the traveler, making this journey difficult and frustrating. Travelers get lost, often fail, and quit. This is not a good model for leading someone into healthy adulthood. Below is a typical maze. It's clear how a person could wander through it indefinitely without finding the center or even getting back outside. In theory a person could get stuck in a maze forever.

Figure 4-Maze

Conversely, a labyrinth is a simple guided path allowing a clear trail to the center and then back out again. Without the confusion and frustration of a maze, a labyrinth offers a subtler, internally focused trip where one learns from the quietness within. Note that after you enter from the bottom(Figure 5), you need merely to follow the path before you and it will lead you into the center and easily back out again.

Figure 5--Labyrinth

The scenario adolescents face as they try to become adults in modern cultures is very much a maze in that they are expected to get through on their own. The maze is what we create when we look at adolescence as "a phase to get through" and an impediment to adult productivity. The maze stirs anger and invites failure along the way, often leading the traveler nowhere at all. Getting stuck is common, which often results in quitting. For our youth, quitting the path is quitting the future.

The universal structures of initiations and rites of passage were built on the principle of the labyrinth: to create a clear and simple path to adulthood without all the negativity, difficulty, and arbitrariness of the maze. This simple (but not necessarily easy) path was created by those who had walked it previously and who would also support and mentor those who followed. The guides were the elders who had completed the process themselves, giving back and passing on their knowledge. Sadly, elder mentors have become almost extinct in this day of forced retirement, moving to warmer climates, and the breakdown of extended families.

The labyrinth represents a trail followed by countless others before, marked carefully for future generations to follow, just as a hazy trail may be marked with rock cairns left by a previous traveler. These trails were monitored and maintained for all to use. An example of this generational process is childbirth. With some obvious medical exceptions, all women have the ability to endure childbirth, and indeed this 'path' has been walked literally billions of times successfully. Thus, women who have had children can model strength and courage for the young mother-to-be. She is following a path walked by countless women, so she can draw comfort from that and know she is not alone in her fears, insecurities and pain.

Today's teens meander down an unmarked trail, the rock-cairn aids dismantled and discarded. They plow ever forward, stumbling into the blocked passages and closed pathways of the maze, looking for signs or clues to the correct direction but not finding them. There are no clear criteria for them to follow or emulate, and they often become lost or take the wrong path.

Adolescence has an often negative image in modern society, but this has not always been the case. Historically, modern adolescent behavior as we have come to expect it has been the exception rather than the rule. There's a reason so many independent and isolated communities throughout history and across the planet all developed a similar approach for helping their adolescents through this difficult coming-of-age period: it worked! Traditional, indigenous cultures did not have the luxury or resources for pursuing and embracing approaches that did not work. Being irresponsible and lazy is a luxury of modern teens only. The universality of these approaches worldwide and historically is an indication of how well they worked and the necessity of providing them in modern times--especially in modern times.

We, the former travelers of adolescence, are bound by love, history, and experience to create clearer paths for our youth, to provide maps for them to follow, and to remodel our mazes into labyrinths. One of the great crimes in modern times has been to steal these practices from our youth, forcing them into the maze and taking away the responsibility and the rewards of walking the time-honored paths to adulthood.

The second greatest crime has been in holding this irresponsibility and lack of guidance against them.

Bret Stephenson

Fourteen

The Religion of Gangs

*Even gang members imagine a future that
doesn't include gangs.*
Greg Boyle – Homeboy Industries

One of the most difficult type of teen to change is one affiliated with a gang, and the more entrenched within the gang mentality the harder it is to convince the teen to resign (if he or she is allowed). I believe this is the result of a couple of dynamics. Even when kids join gangs, at some level they know they will likely be incarcerated because of the illegal activity associated with being in a gang. Basically, where most teens hope never to be locked up, at some level gang members expect it, so they react differently than a kid who never expected to be there. Depending on their age, gang bangers will likely do time in juvenile detention if under 18, with prison or jail a possibility for older kids. For minors, other types of incarceration may include residential treatment centers, boot camps, group homes, ranch settings, alternative schools and more. Related to this is an acceptance of things illegal as a way of life.

Most of the thousands of teens I've worked with do not really like being in trouble, being locked up in any fashion. Indeed, who would? In small settings, like juvenile hall, rival gang members will fight each other and try desperately to protect their unique *set*, their local gang. So for many gang members, getting locked up simply means they just *bang* within the lock-down setting, either as their own specific gang or as a more general means for protection, such as Hispanics vs. Blacks vs. Whites will do in large US prisons where they cannot safely or successfully subcategorize. For many teen gang members, it is more important that they prove their loyalty to the gang by *banging* inside juvenile hall or other program settings than backing off the gang issues and completing their program or time duration. Adherence to the gang overrides individual freedom.

Teens often suffer from a form of denial we call magical thinking. Magical thinking is an amazing tool teens use to feel immortal, to convince themselves that they'll never get arrested, get addicted, become pregnant, or killed in a car accident, for example. Gang members, I have found, typically have magical thinking as well about getting killed or arrested, but once they actually get arrested, their desire to claim homage to their gang kicks in and they *bang* where they are. In a way, it doesn't really matter where they play gang member, just that they do so in the correct way for their gang.

I've come to look at the second reason it is so hard to get gang kids out of that belief system is that the gang becomes the youth's religion, so to speak, his or her most serious attachment or belief system in life, often transcending his or her biological family. And the religion of gangs is, for many kids, a literal conversion of belief, like becoming a born-again Christian or missionary-converted Mormon. This, of course, is because most of them were not born with this belief system, but that is changing with more multiple generations of gang members within a family.

Sadly, more and more kids are born into gangs, brought into the fold by mothers and fathers or other family members who are themselves generational members. These are not "religious" converts as explained above but more similar to families who have long histories of following one belief, such as Catholic or Presbyterian. Sadly, the gang lifestyle and belief system is all they have ever known.

So whether born into the belief or being born-again into the belief, the attachment to the gang becomes intensely serious, worthy of dying for, killing for, or giving up everything else you love for. I can't tell you how many sad and devastated parents I've talked with who watch their sons and daughters head into a belief and values system they can't understand, like generational Catholic parents watching a child convert to the another faith or other system very much different than they are familiar with except this one hurts other people.

And what is ultimately sad for these parents, the ones who don't want their kids to be in gangs, is that their kids not only have converted to another belief system, but this system encourages breaking and disrespecting the law, selling drugs, and advocating violence. This belief system is anti-community, anti-education and very discriminatory. You not only don't like or approve of the other person's faith, but you get to beat them up or shoot them for that age-old feud.

The religion of gangs does not like its members to leave the fold. Where Methodists or Baptists will try desperately to dissuade a person from leaving the faith, they don't forbid it at the cost of violence. Many gangs do not allow for an exit from the gang. "Once in, always in" becomes the mantra. Countless gang kids have told me they would like to get out of their gangs, but if they go back to their neighborhoods that will not be possible. The process of getting into a gang is usually to get *jumped-in*, going through a gauntlet of other gang members who beat you up as a test and pseudo-initiation. Some gangs will allow a member to get *jumped-out* the same way, but not often enough. Some will allow a father-to-be to retire and avoid legal problems, but he will remain affiliated and loyal where he can.

And like any other organized religion, new members are needed. Some denominations go door-to-door looking for converts. Some denominations offer billboard advertising or Sunday radio/TV shows that may attract listeners. The religion of gangs is no different. Rather than approaching your kids over the airways or knocking on a neighbor's door, however, they approach new prospects at schools, arcades, malls, and anywhere kids hang out.

They don't wear ties and tote bibles: they wear $150 tennis shoes and sports logo apparel. Often, they tote guns. They offer protection, not of the spiritual kind but of a literal, physical kind. "Mess with me and my homeboys will get you." The gang's version of heaven? Constant partying with lots of alcohol, drugs, and homegirls to be passed around. If you die, your *homies* will make up R.I.P. T-shirts to glorify your death, then look for revenge by hurting someone else. Gangs take advantage of a teenager's propensity for hedonism, idealism and anarchy. Many teens don't like rules, have an ideal way of looking at the world and tend to follow what's fun versus what is responsible.

Most gang members I've worked with will tell you that the gang becomes their family, both literally and figuratively. Too many of the kids in gangs come from single-parent homes, homes with no healthy fathers. Too often the biological family is in chaos from poverty, addiction or other problems. The streets are dangerous and many youth report joining a gang just to feel safe walking to the market. It actually becomes unsafe to not belong to a gang. If a youth cannot find what he or she is looking for in their family or community to believe in, there is a new family and religion ready to welcome them in. Poor job and future educational prospects also fuel the desire to find a quick, easy way to success.

Another problem related to the religion of gangs is in when we adults try to get gang members to give up the gang lifestyle. Ironically, at this point we are now like the door-to-door missionaries trying to sell their version of "what is right." We adults: parents, youth workers, teachers and counselors, to name a few, are now trying to convert the converted. We have the difficult task of trying to persuade the teen to change his or her belief system, to convert from one religion to another one we feel works better for them. How many people at home on the weekend are actually ever converted by a house visit from a religious missionary or zealot?

I don't know about you, but when religious salespeople come to my door, I politely but firmly tell them to go away, that I'm content with my belief system as it is. I wonder how anyone can hope to just drop in on someone and expect them to change what they've believed in for years or decades. Now we force teens to listen to us proselytize our beliefs onto them. As you can imagine, many youth are not amenable to me telling them that they are wrong, or that what their mom or even gang-related grandmother taught them is wrong.

Faith is the belief in, or devotion to, somebody or something, especially without logical proof. Faith is the cornerstone of any religion, particularly when other beliefs try to tell you why yours is wrong or theirs is better. Lately I've been trying to get the gang kids I work with to tell me specifically why they hate their rival gangs, other than the simple reason they are supposed to. Few youths can elaborate why they have such hatred for another teen who is remarkably similar, when you get down to it. For example, Hispanic rivals in California hate each other on principle, kind of like Catholics and Protestants in Northern Ireland.

But the vast majority of kids cannot tell me why, other than they are supposed to.

Often, I point out to one youth that his enemy is another Hispanic boy, with a mother, aunties and siblings just like him. Maybe they, too, live in a tough and impoverished neighborhood. I point out that this enemy is the same nationality, has the same issues and challenges. At face value, the only real difference may be the tattoo each one is sporting. Most kids say "So what! I hate him and that's that." It reminds me of having grown up with the Cold War where we were programmed to hate Russians out of principle, but in actuality most Russians were simply people trying to get by like most Americans. Much of the animosity was stirred up by a minority of adults.

Often the gang logic for joining fails to hold water. I've known family members, brothers even, who join opposing gangs even though they came from the same neighborhood. I knew a gang member once who complained that he lived in the suburbs and had to take a local bus to the ghetto to hang out with his fellow gang members. There's a small rural town in Nevada where two of the same Hispanic gang set up shop. Since they have no natural rivals, they have resorted to fighting each other for territory, bragging rights and so on. Gangs who come from the South will start new gangs in the North, trying to expand their market and territory. Also, setting up gangs in a place like rural Nevada kind of detracts from the argument that they have to join for safety against historical rivals or that they come from an urban environment with no other options.

There are now more than a million youth gang members in America, plenty to qualify as a religion. They are carrying their word to new locations, other countries, with a passion and zeal to rival Christian missionaries. It is said the American Crip gang has more firepower than the Italian mafia. They pursue nonbelievers like the Inquisition. The religion of gangs is firmly established, and will likely continue to grow until we adults give teens something better to believe in.

The religion of gangs has its church in the streets and the ghettos, even in the suburbs and ranch towns. Their membership is growing while real church attendance continues to drop. More teens are converted each year in spite of the inherent dangers. I think we have to ask ourselves what is it we are not providing to these youth and why they keep joining such a dangerous and destructive belief system. We need to lure them away from such activity with our own actions and behavior, as preaching to them tends to fall on deaf ears. In essence, we need to give them something healthier to believe in.

Fifteen

Prisoners of War

People just don't know what civilian prisoners of war are.
Gene Green

As an adolescent counselor, I spend a lot of time trying to get teens to change their negative belief systems, or change their thinking errors. Of course, this is what we adults believe is often the problem with a certain girl or boy. One of the flaws we've succumbed to in America is in misreading the rebelliousness of adolescence as an inherently negative thing. A large part of adolescence is that the teens test their new beliefs and ideas on the realty of the adult world. For teens, trying on new identities, beliefs and behaviors is like trying on a new style of clothes: they've got to see how it fits, how others react and respond to them in this new way.

If we just tell them their *style* is wrong, often they cling harder to the new belief that it is fine--great, in fact! It seems the harder we chase them, the faster they run away. In modern times we have made the process of testing wrong, not the test itself. We've invented boot camps, residential treatment centers, youth detention and other processes to try and break the adolescent spirit into submission. We mistakenly believe it is easier to fight adolescence and squeeze it into submission than to work with the process.

I've spent a lot of time with teens that are incarcerated in some way or the other. Many are in residential treatment programs, juvenile detention, group-homes and so on with probation departments to make sure they stay there. I also spend time with teens that are free to come and go in those residential settings. Some work off-campus, get extended home passes with family, and so on. Interestingly, I've seen many parallels between the kids who are always locked up and teens that were but act and talk like they still are. Often, they simply do not know what to do with personal freedom.

I believe this is because the free teens still feel somewhat controlled and confined emotionally and culturally like their incarcerated counterparts, except with more access to regular society. Nobody seems to understand them, even at 18, 19 or 24, as adolescence keeps lingering on in America's age-arbitrary system of promotion to adulthood by collecting birthdays. Recall the rite of passage system had teens earning their way into adulthood regardless of their age. More and more, teens keep talking and acting to me like prisoners of war, figuratively locked up for their beliefs and actions and treated as less than accepted citizens.

Why prisoners of war? They feel they are kept from fully engaging as equals in the adult world until into their 20's. They are shackled by mind-numbing minimum wage jobs that offer little challenge or growth, except to help make money for the adults. They are hand-cuffed by the declining efficiency of schools. They are treated as less than equals, bound by age and laws with no recourse for being mature and responsible at an early age. Overall, they are punished for often just doing what they are supposed to: testing boundaries.

As I pondered this metaphor of adolescents as prisoners of war, a couple of things struck me. Depending on whether the prisoners of war are your own or your enemy's determines what you expect or demand of them. For example, if our own people are prisoners, we fully expect and encourage them to escape and resist their captors. Indeed, if they don't we might consider them cowards or even traitors. We expect them to resist interrogation and make elaborate plans to escape. We expect them to be as uncooperative as possible as long as they can.

But if the prisoner of war happens to be your enemy, the rules and dynamics change. Now we expect complete cooperation. We expect to be told what we want. We can make them do what we wish. If necessary, we can use physical means and even torture to get what we want. After all, they are the enemy.

Modern teens have all the freedom and luxuries of the 21st century; yet complain incessantly about their situation as second-class citizens. Because we hold the teen propensity to challenge authority against them, they feel inherently wrong and often unsupported or even alienated. They've become prisoners, at least in their minds, of their own society. If they resist, they are punished even harder. If they give in, they are not risking and taking chances that help them grow into adulthood.

As their *prison guards* we adults have to remember what it was like for us as teens. Most parents I've met seem to have forgotten their own antics and teen mistakes, coming down hard on their own children as this next generation continues the pattern. I remember what it was like to be told my choice of clothes were wrong, that my choice of car not logical, or my girlfriend not pretty enough. I remember getting in trouble for many things: breaking curfew and lying to my parents. I remember getting away with much more than I ever got caught for.

I came out of adolescence a good person, I believe, not because I was forced into it, but because I was led into doing good. First by the overall hardworking values around me and secondly because of the mistakes I endured and lessons I learned from them.

Teens often over exaggerate things, as almost any parent can attest. But they also often feel like second-class citizens, not really listened to, with too few freedoms and not enough voice in their lives. Thus, they will sometimes lapse into a "poor me" mindset but also a resistant one. They resist our of principle. They often create an Us vs Them mentality pitting all youth against all adults. This is a feeling they often have in which they want or need to *escape* from, and that they are being overly controlled and want to end that.

Not everyone learns the right lesson from an experience. But stopping everyone from having their chance to make a good decision, or get a second chance, learn to apologize, or accept responsibility for their actions makes subservient citizens, or prisoners of war in a teen's mind. Giving our teens the opportunity to try on their new identities and personas without judgment, while holding them accountable for their actions will create stronger and healthier adults, and like anyone who is treated with some respect, they may work with us and not feel they need an escape.

Sixteen

Persistence vs. Futility

A little more persistence, a little more effort, and what seemed hopeless failure may turn to glorious success.
Elbert Hubbard

When goals become unexpectedly difficult, the dilemma thus lies in reconciling the opposing requirements of goal persistence and goal disengagement.
Nils. Jostmann – Sander L. Koole

If I had to take credit for anything in my teen career, I suppose it would include coming into the field with no theory or attachment to how I thought the teen field should be. Indeed, coming into the field from a Fortune 500 corporate job with no training, experience or education, I laugh now at how bad I was on my first day at work in which I gave myself a 'D' on my personal report card.

I've tried to take lessons I picked up along my own path and apply them to my work with high-risk adolescents, such as 'follow what works and let go of what doesn't' and 'know your product.' While a number of people (all grownups) struggle with the flavor of my work, I have simply followed what works best with my clientele. I sometimes joke to people that if I had learned that what would help prevent a teen from self-destructing was to recite the alphabet backwards in Portuguese while standing on his/her head in the corner, that is what I'd be preaching.

In my Fortune 500 corporate past-life I was taught you couldn't know your product well enough. When I tried to overlay that understanding onto my growing teen career, largely I found that few people in the youth industry seemed to know what adolescence was supposed to look like on a perfect day. I spent years trying to understand how adolescence should look or operate. After working with teens from more than 100 countries, I knew the American model I was so familiar with was not the rule worldwide, but the exception.

Few other professionals could tell me, for they didn't know either. America, as I came to understand it, has the most broken model of adolescence on the planet, and I think most of that is due to adult behavior, not teens'. Much of what I learned in that journey is documented in my first book, *From Boys to Men: Spiritual Rites of Passage in an Indulgent Age.* My continued growth and understanding of adolescence if further documented in my second book *The Undercurrents of Adolescence: Tracking the Evolution of Modern Adolescence and Delinquency Through Classic Cinema*

As a former boy and now a man, one of the other great tools I found was to take what I was learning about myself, or what I had just experienced in some workshop, sweat lodge or drum circle, for example, and then ponder how it might work with the teens I was involved with. Being bold at heart and always curious to add to my teen tool belt with tips and tricks, I would try these new/ancient approaches on teens and monitor the results. To be fair, I also tried all the usual psychobabble approaches as well, but the kids resisted those more and I simply got fewer results than with more archetypal ones.

Typically, if the attempt worked, I'd add it to my repertoire. If not, I'd swallow my pride and embarrassment then ask the teens in question why they felt it hadn't worked.

I'd try to refine the process until it worked, or let it go as a good idea that looked good on paper but didn't manifest in real life as expected. Examples of projects or models others have been tried that looked good on paper but failed the reality test are Scared Straight, Just Say NO, and D.A.R.E.. Basically, Scared Straight was supposed to scare delinquent boys from wanting to go to prison but in actuality created a challenge or dare to do just that. Essentially, what happens when you tell a bad-boy NOT to do something? Yep, he usually does it.

D.A.R.E. (Drug Abuse Resistance & Education) is an effort to educate grade school youth about the evils of drug abuse. Looks good on paper. Sadly, the actual impact of teaching kids about drugs at an early age has backfired as former D.A.R.E. youth do more drugs and at an earlier age then most of their counterparts. Would you prefer your 10-year-old know everything about drugs or nothing about them? Which one would snort cocaine or smoke methamphetamines? A kid who knows nothing about the processor everything about it? My experience has been the more naïve the better until a bit later when adolescence hits and natural curiosity becomes a more pressing concern. This is a conversation that would ideally come from the parents, but more and more as families break down and we relinquish more parenting to schools and agencies, strangers are teaching our kids.

America's official drug policy since the 80s stemmed from a comment made by President Reagan's wife for kids to "Just say no" to drugs, which has proven over and over to be short sighted and ineffective. Just Say No is contrary to adolescent defiance and creates an inherent challenge. It also often fails against peer pressure from the teen's friends or social group. And frankly, it is a weak and unenforceable policy, costing about $20 billion each year just to tell kids No. Just Say No is not real in the world of teens. How many of us adults did zero experimenting as teens?

Kids start with what they know and move onward from there: the gateway process. Many of us see our folks smoke cigarettes or have occasional drinks, for example. We see (normally) as children that not much drama comes from those rather benign behaviors. Then, as we see how our own experimentation has gone or witnessed our friends trying other things, sometimes we expand our usage to other things. Thus, it stands to reason why we don't want to tell young kids about hard drugs, because we speed up the learning curve.

As a kid of the 1960s I was deeply impacted by the overdose deaths of American rock legends Jim Morrison, Jimi Hendrix and Janis Joplin. Also, after my very first middle school party at age 13 where we mostly listened to music and tried to get the nerve to ask girls to dance, afterward the host of the party died when he later tried huffing model airplane glue inside a plastic bag. He passed out with the plastic bag on his head and suffocated. Those were the lessons that actually helped keep me away from hard drugs and stay in the lighter experimenting level even past my teen years. The reality of my friend's death was more immediate to scaring me away from drugs than the abstract of my music idols I didn't know.

Interestingly, D.A.R.E. continues and there are attempts are reincarnating a new Scared Straight in a naïve attempt to get a different outcome with the next generation of youth. The System continues to pursue models of drug resistance, gang preventions or other models largely in spite of the fact many of them are not working. This is what leads me to the topic of this particular essay.

One of the abstract concepts I've been pondering the past couple of years is this: what or where is the line between *persistence* and *futility*. In other words, how much is enough?

When was it time to throw in the towel, or looked at the other way, did we give up too soon? When does chasing a dream become just that—a dream? But then what about all the success stories about persistence paying off? No one can tell a person when to give up or not—only the individual knows that.

I apply this persistence vs. futility concept to both my teens and the teen programs I work under. To mix metaphors, how long do we try to force square-peg kids into round-hole programs? When do I give up on this one boy: six times, twelve times, 37 times? Why do we waste billions of dollars on programs like Just Say NO that Just Haven't Worked?

There is no answer to the questions, I've found. Stories abound of the waiter who wants to be an actor who still hasn't made it at 45. Or the minor league ball player still hoping to break into the Big Leagues. Others show where persistence pays off, and who knows after you quit that the next time might not have been the magic turning point?

Mad Men star Jon Hamm was 36 when he got that big break. Harrison Ford had minor roles like in *American Graffiti,* and was a full time carpenter when George Lucas brought him back at age 36 for *Star Wars.* Samuel L. Jackson had earlier roles but got his big break in *Pulp Fiction* at age 46!

I started pondering this point when I was working with older teens that had younger siblings. Often, the older teen was destroying the family, breaking hearts and wasting precious resources a single mom could ill-afford to waste. Two months, ten months, two years later--when do we let go of trying to save one kid who doesn't seem to want help at the expense of the others? Often, while we blindly try to help someone who doesn't want help we allow other kids to fall into the negative patterns. I'm reminded of the triage scenes in the TV show *MASH* where initial decisions had to be made for wounded soldiers based on who could be saved or not.

Sometimes the resources and time needed to save one person meant four others would not be saved.

Some of the best youth workers I've met, or know of, are successful largely due to their incredible persistence and energy. Great youth workers like Father Greg Boyle at Homeboy Industries in Los Angeles or Geoffrey Canada in Harlem made their own programs to fit their kids' needs, not make the kids fit outdated models. Like so many gifted and persistent athletes, artists and musicians, there are countless brilliant youth workers out there with great ideas for helping kids who never get discovered and make the "big time."

But great youth workers do not operate for long in models they know don't work. They'll either break through and start a good program or quit the field and go elsewhere. This is happening more and more with America's Evidence Based Programming dogma in youth treatment that basically prohibits creativity while almost mandating existing models only. Similarly, the trend to standardize education is inhibiting good teachers from doing what they are good at—being creative, in favor of trying to have every classroom be the same. Great youth workers will not beat their heads against the wall, to mix metaphors one more time. That's a sign of futility, after their persistence has worn thin.

Seventeen

Information Overload or Overdose?

"One of the effects of living with electric information is that we live habitually in a state of information overload. There's always more than you can cope with".
Marshall McLuhan- 1967

There's a paradox behind why a logical anti-drug campaign like D.A.R.E. (Drug Awareness & Resistance Education) has failed to live up to its common-sense approach: too much information about drugs too early in life takes away some of the fear or mystique of drugs that actually prevents many children from experimenting early on. Literally educating children about drugs increases the chances they will indulge in them. It is preferable to me, and against that initial logic, to keep them in the dark, because young children are not prone to smoking and ingesting substances they know little or nothing about. I believe that is even simpler logic.

This modern propensity to give information to our kids is backfiring in a number of ways. The media's mantra of the "public's right to know" mostly sells their products but often gives kids more information than they really need. In modern times, we are definitely an information-based society. Hundreds of channels are offered through cable TV companies. The Internet was built specifically to disseminate information. Newspapers and TV news bombard households with a never-ending supply of drama, as do soap operas and reality TV. We keep thinking that if we ever get enough information, we'll be better off somehow. For decades, movies were made for families; now we have to rate them so parents can determine how much questionable content to allow our kids to view.

Part of the problem with this mindset is that too much information kills curiosity in teens. Adolescents, as we all know, often believe they know everything already. Offering them every bit of adult life and understanding on a media platter adds to their belief that they don't need to learn anything more, and kills their curiosity about learning overall. More and more every year, I see teens becoming less and less curious about life and our culture. Part of this relates to the need for adults to model behavior that teens actually want to emulate. Historically, teens have always wanted to become like the adults around them, because those adults had all the (perceived) perks in life. And of course the adolescent mind loves to see just the funs parts of adult life without recognizing the deep responsibilities most of us pay for those rewarding moments and possessions.

A few years ago I came to see curiosity as a developmental aspect of adolescence, like puberty, search for identity, individuation, and egocentricity, to name a few. Developmental challenges, or stages, are those aspects we all go through in order to grow. Adolescence is the second greatest developmental growth spurt we humans go through, second only to birth-2 years old. Successful completion of the developmental stages helps ensure a youth will develop into a mature and responsible adult. Failure to grow through the developmental stages is just that: failure to grow. This often leads to those 45-year-old folks we know who act 14.

Native cultures, who I've explained before in *From Boys to Men: Spiritual Rites of Passage in an Indulgent Age,* dealt successfully with teens for millennia without having to resort to incarceration or medication. They knew, or learned, how to use teen curiosity as a lure to get teens to join the adult club. How? By initially keeping *healthy secrets* about important life aspects until adolescence and focusing largely on survival training prior to that. Children raised in indigenous cultures are taught how to survive, first and foremost. It doesn't do any good to promote a youth forward who can't cook, kill, tan hides, track animals, garden, or make tools and weapons. Modern survival training may have changed to reading, writing and arithmetic, but the concept still holds true.

Important aspects of adult life such as procreation, birth control, parenting, relationships, creation, religion and so on were usually NOT offered to children or teens until they were involved in their initiation into adulthood. By withholding these critical pieces of adulthood, the teens were forced to join the adult club to access this information. Native cultures all over the world used this same process to keep youth curious, and to use that curiosity to lure them forward into growth. Keeping healthy secrets from children also prevented creating the teen we all fear: the one who knows everything!

Modern kids are inundated with information. Indeed, our current times are called the Information Age. Youth acquire an understanding early in life about marriage and divorce, pre-marital sex, drugs, porn, politics and more. While these are not inherently negative topics, they are not critically important for young people to know and sadly we Americans do not model the best of each topic: America leads the world in divorce rate, incarceration, teen violence and a host of other dubious distinctions. 85% of all sex portrayed on American TV is to unmarried couples, teaching that pre-marital sex is all right and that marriage is not sexy. How do I expect my daughter to 'wait until she's married' when every book and movie she sees suggests the opposite?

Each year the schools struggle more and more with engaging kids in class. Each year I see less understanding of how our culture works from teens who have turned off their curiosity because they've "seen it all." For example, none of the African-American boys in either of my recent process groups knew what the Emancipation Proclamation was about, when it happened, or how it affected them. Their understanding of Black progress begins with Martin Luther King and the Civil Rights Movement, who are now more often being referred to by teens as something that happened "back in the day." They have been so bored and uninvolved in school they've failed to learn this and other critical pieces of their heritage. But they know everything about drugs, gangs and sex....

Back in the days of wholesome American TV shows like *Leave it to Beaver, Father Knows Best and My Three Sons*, kids did not have much inkling of how the adult world worked. Adult behavior was withheld from them and youth were safely naïve. If you think about much of teen behavior, it is an attempt to act as an adult. Teens today are in too much of a hurry to grow up, and we as a culture seem to believe that we should expose them to all aspects of adult life and expedite that growth. We're only teens for a few years and then adults for decades. We can't totally blame teens for knowing too much when we hand it to them on a platter. If you're tired of kids who know everything, keep them in the dark a bit longer; it won't kill them.

Modern youth carefully witness and process the poor behavior of the adults around them, from real life drama to TV shows and movies. From this they often become cynical about the adult world of lifelong work, paying taxes, bills, responsibility, environmental problems, overpopulation, wars, political corruption and all the other aspects of grownup life. Not all adult aspects are negative but the point is they see these obstacles early on and choose to checkout in video games, social media, and other distractions.

Can a teen, or adult for that matter, handle the massive amount of information coming at them in current times? Students are beginning to lose basic skills like spelling because they rely on spell-check to fix their writing. Multitasking has been proven to be less effective than focusing on one topic at a time. Retention of information is declining because the 'answer' is at anyone's fingertips and students don't need to memorize information anymore. And the sheer amount of information coming at any of us is astronomical, and growing by the minute.

The top four 2016 web sites used in the US are, in order, Google, Yahoo, Facebook and YouTube. Two are straight search engines to find information and answers. 128 million Americans tap into YouTube daily as it disseminates a broad variety of information, including tutorials on how to do almost anything. Google and Yahoo serve over 350 million Americans daily trying to get answers and info. The sheer volume is staggering. How can we expect young people to discriminate what is important, truthful and useful in all that data? And can we really hold it against the natural curiosity of youth to investigate the darker side of life in all this free information?

I don't see an easy answer for this issue. I tried very hard when my daughter was growing up to limit her access to public TV, commercials, and the consumerism prevalent in the US. That worked very well until her first week in middle school where she took the school bus and got an undesired education that pretty much dismantled all the hard parenting work I had put into trying to keep all this information overload from reaching her. Like most youth, she embraced the social media, multitasking, and relying on the Internet to teach her. Interestingly, as she has matured into her early twenties, she has left social media completely and now focuses more on each individual task at hand, so perhaps she learned the flaw in her peers' continuing reliance on such delivery systems.

That makes me believe that such efforts as mine to insulate her from much of life's deeper and darker issues until she was a teen paid off in the long run. Somehow she has let go of the information avalanche coming at her and become more discriminate in what she deems important for her new adult life.

The growth in the internet, 24-hour television and mobile phones means that we now receive five times as much information every day as we did in 1986. Every day the average person produces six newspapers worth of information compared with just two and a half pages 24 years ago – nearly a 200-fold increase. Every day more information now crosses the Internet than the sum of all history combined. Google handles 4 million search queries every minute, and in that same minute:

- Facebook users share nearly 2.5 million pieces of content.
- Twitter users tweet nearly 300,000 times.
- Instagram users post nearly 220,000 new photos.
- YouTube users upload 72 hours of new video content.
- Apple users download nearly 50,000 apps.
- Email users send over 200 million messages.
- Amazon generates over $80,000 in online sales.

The San Diego Supercomputer Center estimates "the sum of media asked for and delivered to consumers on mobile devices and to their homes would take more than 15 hours a day to see or hear. That volume is equal to 6.9 million-

million gigabytes of information, or a daily consumption of nine DVDs worth of data per person per day."

It is estimated that 100,000 words, about one fourth the size of Tolstoy's *War and Peace* pass by American eyes every day. And while these statistics are staggering and sobering, they keep growing exponentially each year, each month, each week, each day, each hour.

When I was a kid there was not a movie I could not see. Sure, I may not understand all the adult dynamics going on but I waited patiently for the action scenes. I remember my mother's discomfort at the sensual introduction to *Thunderball,* one of the earlier James Bond films. Now the US and many other countries have to supply ratings or suggestions for what is deemed age-appropriate for our children to watch.

For example, our current PG-13 stands for Parental Guidance and youth under 13 are advised not to watch the film. This list includes films such as *Harry Potter, Jurassic Park, Men in Black,* and even the cartoon *Brave Little Toaster.* More interesting to me though, are the wide variety of warnings that prepare the young viewer for what is coming. Here are a number of separate PG-13 movie labels common in the US:

- Rude humor and drug references
- Language, sexual content, drug references
- Sexual content, teen partying, language
- Rude humor
- Matter dealing with sexual issues
- Suggestive dialogue
- Intense sequences of science fiction terror
- Intense sequences of violence and action
- Disturbing thematic material, violence, sexuality, and brief drug use
- Violence, drinking, language, blood and gore, some thematic elements, stylized action sequences and a scene of rape

- Sequences of intense sci-fi action and violence throughout, and brief suggestive content
- For irreverent humor throughout
- Sexual material including some suggestive dialogue
- Language, sexual content and brief drug references
- Brief sexual humor
- Some sensuality and language

If I was a young teen again, these 'warnings' would actually serve to *entice* me to check them out. Who decides that a 13-year-old is mature enough to handle such input? As soon as the US came up with 'R' rated Restricted movies for over 18 only without a parent, we teen boys began sneaking in to see what was so taboo. The new system only served to lead us into temptation hoping to see naked women and graphic violence. With teens, they are often drawn to the taboo.

Our challenge as elders and parents is to help youth navigate this torrent of information and try to sift out the important parts, and encourage them to show some self-restraint in their on-line and media activities. We are now literally being subjected to more information that we can actually read, view or even process with no respite in sight. The Information Drug has become as powerful and addictive as any other distraction, and while technology temporarily serves our youth for answers and research I fear our teens (and many adults) are ending up serving the technology instead.

Eighteen

Attention Deficit

Everyone I know has attention deficit, and they say it with great pride. It's a bad time to be right.
Joni Mitchell

This essay is not about one of the most common topics and problems associated with teens, particularly boys: Attention Deficit Disorder (ADD) and/or Attention Deficit with Hyperactivity Disorder (ADHD). There have been volumes written about the effects of teens and other children who suffer from an inability to pay attention. This malady seems to particularly frustrate modern adults more than our predecessors, who I don't believe had more leisure time than we currently do but knew the value of giving attention to youth who need it. America currently medicates almost 5% of every boy with Ritalin or other mood-altering drug in an effort to get boys more attentive and to sit still longer.

Over a century ago G. Stanley Hall, the first writer to bring the new concept of modern adolescence into light, pointed out way back in 1904 that, "Constant muscular activity was natural for the child, and, therefore, the immense effort of the drillmaster teachers to make children sit still was harmful and useless." He followed up in 1906 by commenting "Abundance and vigor of automatic movements are desirable, and even a considerable degree of restlessness is a good sign in young children." Indeed, one of the initial causes leading to ADD/ADHD problems is trying to make boys sit still and be quiet all day. Anyone who has worked with boys knows this is not in our nature. Recent studies have shown that one in seven boys will be diagnosed as ADHD by the time they finish high school, with 10% of every school boy in the US on medication.

But one of the biggest problems facing teens in modern times is the lack of attention given to them overall-a *deficit of attention* they need to learn from and be healthy. There are countless statistics available to show you how little direct attention many youngsters get from parents, poor eating habits, how much time they spend watching TV and playing escapist video games, and so on. More often than not, both parents work outside the home, considered a modern economic necessity but nevertheless creating even more chasms between youth and adults.

As an adolescent counselor I've heard thousands of individual and family stories. Usually, these are the stories teens and their parents tell me in an effort to explain why or how the teen's behavior got to where it is. While every story is unique, too many of them are remarkably similar. Often when meeting a teen for the first time I tell them I can ask about five questions and guesstimate much of their lives from those few answers. Usually, the teen is amazed that I can often do it.

This is because so many issues and dynamics in teen dysfunction are similar from family to family. Basically, teens do not just head out of control without a reason. They may experiment with drugs or alcohol, or maybe sex, but a lot of the time the experimentation is enough without heading into a self-destructive mode. Nothing leads a teen into trouble like one not getting enough quality attention.

Simply put, teen misbehavior is usually a result of too little effective parenting and/or attention from the parents or other primary caregivers. A very high percentage of the thousands of teens I've worked with, especially boys, have not had attentive fathers or other parental figures. Just when teens need the most supervision and interaction with caregivers, so many parents struggle with the inability or unwillingness to talk about sex, drugs, school, and other issues critical to teens.

Many teens I've worked with have both parents, but investigation almost always shows that even if there is no serious dysfunction in the home like alcoholism or child abuse, teens will stray toward the dark side if their parents are inattentive to the teen's needs and changing world.

Parents I commonly work with saw no reason, for example, to question the new tattoo their 14-year-old boy came home with, or to understand that the tattoo was gang related. These parents fail to notice missing cigarettes or liquor at home, or that their teen is not home in bed, or that their grades have dropped precipitously in the last couple of months. They may have changed their group of friends or who they associate with. Wearing a common gang color exclusively often gets ignored.

This inattention is commonly explained away to me by parents who believe that adolescence is a phase, and that most teen drama will end on its own without adult or parental intervention. This belief is convenient for inattentive parents who have other things to do than get intimately involved in their teens' lives. Often, for working parents, adolescence is considered an inconvenience, affecting their work and private lives with its demands. Like most problems though, ignore them and the problems continue and often get worse.

The best functioning teens I've run across come from attentive parents, adults who are involved intimately in their children's lives. They go to the trouble to know how their child is doing daily in school, speak regularly with teachers, assist with homework, check up on sleepovers and other situations that teens notoriously disguise from parents.

Sure, teens are notorious for getting in trouble because they are bored, or because of peer pressure encouraging them to do something they know they shouldn't. Bored teens are not difficult to notice; they are the ones who are demanding attention. We are all aware of the fact that people will try to gain attention by either positive or negative behavior.

As someone who has spent most of the past 30 years with teens who got in trouble of some sort, I've seen over and over how so many teens tried to engage their parents or other loved ones in positive ways, only to fail to garner the attention they need. So when inattentive parents or teachers do not recognize the positive attention-seeking behavior in front of them, they will soon have to deal with the negative attention-seeking behavior that comes soon afterward.

Bored teens will slip in school, push parents' buttons just for fun, and draw attention to themselves in a variety of nonproductive ways. In simple terms, the teen is saying "kiss me or kick me, but don't ignore me."

So get involved with your teen's daily life. Don't settle for pat answers like school was OK today, or the movie date was fine. Remember how much stuff happened to you every day in school or how awkward or tense dates could be. Chances are good your teens will tell you not to bother, that they are fine without all of your attention.

Don't believe them. They're saying what they think they're supposed to say, but deep down, they crave your attention. Some part of them needs your attention in spite of their recent behavior or comments to the contrary. Remember, life is both defined and denied by lack of attention. Rather than attention deficit with teens, how about we try *attention abundance* with them.

Nineteen

Square Pegs and Round Holes

"Here's to the crazy ones, the misfits, the rebels, the troublemakers, the round pegs in the square holes."
Steve Jobs

Adolescents are adolescents are adolescents. George W. Bush was one, as was Plato, Einstein, Attila the Hun, Marie Antoinette, Kafka, Gandhi, Elvis and every other adult to ever walk the earth. Even animals struggle with adolescence--pups and kittens trying to leave the den too early, trying to hunt on their own, leaving the safety of the den or burrow. You'd think that after so many thousands or even millions of years, after countless generations and so many billions of teens passing through, we'd be used to the process by now.

America leads the world in adolescent dysfunction, yet I've learned that the great majority of the time teens have very good reasons for why and how they act. It may not be appropriate behavior, but it does make sense. The continuing breakdown of the typical family unit, which helped create the need for foster care, preschool and after school programs in the first place, has modern teens in most modern cultures struggling with shifting societal values. Add to that the loss of initiations, the longest adolescence in history, and the least actual teen responsibility on the planet, and it is clear the current model is not effective.

For three decades I have been working with at-risk and high-risk teens, although if you follow teen statistics you've probably come to join me in thinking every teen in America is at-risk nowadays. Many teen models and/or programs continue to try and break the spirit of adolescence, trying to get those "square peg" kids we're too familiar with into the System's "round hole" mentality.

Countless youth I've known have tried to explain how they just don't fit the one and only model open to them. The most damaging aspect of this trend has been in the shame, blame, guilt and judgment they inherit with all that 'failure.' The success I enjoy with bad boys and girls comes from a simple philosophy. Each youth is an individual, not a number, a DSM diagnosis, or a case file. If the program doesn't fit the youth, then I try desperately to make the program fit the youth. If the square peg doesn't fit into the round hole, change the shape of the hole!

I've come to believe that most *programs* don't work. This is because by the time they are thought up, designed and developed, written and eventually funded, then finally implemented, quite often the original problem has shifted. Also, most nonprofits, in spite of their altruistic tendencies, are competing with other similar programs for limited funding. This does not create a truly cooperative and collaborative interagency dynamic. Programs seldom have any reciprocation built into them for services provided, which is not the way of the world. Finally, they seldom have the support of the community overall—they may not be neglected but many communities have little day-to-day involvement with nonprofit organizations.

Often a single program is developed and numerous different types of youth are forced into fitting the one model, rather than a model being developed for the clientele. Finally, there is a sad yet powerful inherent double bind in service work: it is not really in any program or agency's best interest to prevent or cure the problems leading to their existence. If the problems bringing clients through the doors, and funding in the mail, stop coming, a lot of social service workers will be unemployed.

Take myself, for example. As an adolescent specialist, my goal is to either Prevent or Cure the delinquent and other negative behavior in modern teens. However, if I ever really pull that off somehow, think how many social workers, probation officers, therapists, group home staff, juvenile detention workers, court staff, and so on will lose their jobs. Thus, it is very common for an unconscious sabotage to manifest in the form of good lip service but mediocre follow-through.

At a deep, unconscious level many workers understand that if they are truly successful in solving their particular problem, they will have nothing to do. A cancer surgeon's greatest fear, probably unconsciously, is a cure for cancer. Programs, by their very nature, need the problem to continue so the program can keep going. This dynamic is very prevalent elsewhere: law enforcement who wants to stop crime but if they ever do, then we have a lot of unemployed police officers.

A similar example of this lies in how many high schools grade themselves by how many students they get enrolled in college. But they don't include the data on the continual failure and exodus of students throughout the college years to be part of their success rate. In the US, college freshman drop out of college consistently decade after decade at a 50% rate in the first fall semester. By the end of everything, about 30% of Americans have a Bachelor's degree. But that also implies a 70% failure rate on the college track.

I work mostly with the kids who don't fit the college track in spite of efforts by the school to tell them that is their best and only hope of getting ahead. Most of the youth I work with will end up tradesmen, truck drivers, construction workers and so on. If everyone completes college, then who will tune up our cars, roof our homes, fix our streets? While I am a fan of continuing education, I've come to see that not everyone is built for college but might do much better in a vocational or technical school.

Some people have called me 'enabling' for working with the kids rather than making them always fit my adult needs. Nothing could be further from the truth. Thousands of boys will tell you about my firm boundaries and expectations. My finesse comes from not forcing the adolescent to fight me, but from giving him or her another way to look at success. The adolescent spirit cannot and should not be squelched. Adolescence is about growth, about change, and we adults and parents should be using every resource we have to help youth succeed, not just keep proving how bad they are.

What does this get you? Respect! And if a teen respects you, then you've both got a chance to succeed. When he or she sees you taking grief from the System for them, they'll match that energy back. Do you really want your teen to succeed, or just follow orders? Should adolescence be difficult out of principle, or as smooth a path as we can make for them? If you keep running into the adolescent 'brick wall,' perhaps it's time to try a new path with a different shape.

Many, many youth workers I've worked with fall into the mindset of essentially proving to themselves that a particular teen, or teens, is wrong or bad. They delight in telling me how my teen got in trouble or what antics he was up to lately. My response is always the same: so what? With my high-risk kids, or even easier kids, finding things they are doing wrong is a given; it's part of the process. If these staff really want to impress me, find something the teen is doing right, or if not that, then what he or she is doing wrong less often. For teens to succeed, we have to really want them to, not just catch them at incorrect behaviors.

Literally, it is not that difficult to turn a round hole into a square hole. In woodworking, one big challenge is to make a square hole in the middle of a board. However, if you drill a round hole the same diameter of the overall hole you need, then you have only to chisel out the corners. Similarly, I don't think it is impossible to change the way we work with and look at teens. Many programs just need refinement, or a more open approach and flexibility. Each agency or organization needs to look at their model and see how to better make it fit their actual target audience.

For example, I was called in to assist a new private school that was struggling. They had a great model of open classrooms, cool teachers, and expected to be a very creative school. However, being new to the area, they did not get a lot of private high-end students but ended up with many teens, mostly boys, who had been suspended or even expelled from local schools.

When they put these wild boys in this holistic, alternative setting with no male teachers or role models of any kind, the boys literally disrupted the school into chaos. The school was stuck in trying to make resistant kids fit a model designed for highly motivated students. They didn't adjust the shape of the program, or "hole," and closed down after just a couple years.

I was recently helping a group of people in California try to start a mentoring program for teens. There are some motivated and talented people involved, but none of them have ever worked with teens, and just because a person is good at some skill doesn't mean they can teach it or make it teen friendly. They wanted to reach at-risk kids in the community but have not tapped into the schools to get their input or support. The program model is fun, but wrongly geared toward younger kids as arts and crafts which won't pull in the older teens.

By also coming up with a $200 cost for a day's activities, they failed to realize their target group could not afford that much money and they attracted wealthy kids who just wanted something new to do. They still haven't adjusted their approach, or even their name and look to appeal to teens, so that part is failing. They have changed the shape of their holes a bit as they realized the 12-year-olds they were getting were happy to mentor younger kids, so they altered part of the model to follow this success.

But they are further than ever from their goal of helping at-risk teens, especially the older ones. For that to happen, they need to pass the teen 'cool' test. This means the logo and name need to appeal to teens. Basically, in my experience, if a teen won't wear your logo or slogan on a t-shirt they won't walk in the door. The program activities need to be things older teens are interested in like video and music production, gaming or game programming, and so on. The group needs a crash course on adolescence but they've had problems even getting all the adults into the same room due to varying schedules. So while they may have interested people, if they cannot commit, a key ingredient with teens, then they need to reevaluate their players. I've even pulled back on my consulting because there are no teens for me to consult on. Basically, they had a model that did not adjust or adapt to the kids present.

So while they have failed on one hand to reach their target population due to lack of knowledge and experience with teens, they are adapting to the younger kids who are mostly children of wealthy parents who can afford a one-day luxury for their children.

You absolutely cannot know enough about adolescence. You can't get enough training or read enough books. Teens have changed dramatically over the decades of the past century or so, thus it also becomes important to understand the history of teen issues in modern times and how they developed. They are such a diverse group because of the developmental differences and challenges of each year. The difference in a 13-year-old and a 15-year-old is huge compared to the difference between a seven- and nine-year old or even a 27-to-29 year-old. I cover this cultural shift of teens through the past century in my second book, *The Undercurrents of Adolescence: Tracking the Evolution of Modern Adolescence and Delinquency Through Classic Cinema.*

You can't throw a broad drug abuse model at teens, for example, because there are a number of different reasons different types of teens might use drugs. For example, an honor student might use some stimulants to stay up studying for an important test, then need some marijuana or something to bring him/her down enough to actually sleep for the test. Escapist kids often use psychedelics or hallucinogens to leave this reality for a different one. Angry kids use drugs to rebel or perhaps blow off steam. Class clown personalities often use different combinations of drugs to keep their humor changing. Some kids use only one substance and others use the whole spectrum of drug/alcohol options.

The point is that to be effective, you have to understand the needs and differences of the kids you are working with and try to fit your model to them, rather than every teen who takes drugs being processed into the same punitive group setting. The same process should be followed with delinquent behavior, school problems, and so on. Obviously it is impossible to literally invent a custom approach for every teen, but you need your model to be flexible and expandable based on future needs or changes in who shows up.

So, based on this metaphor of trying to fit Square Peg kids into Round Hole models and programs, it is easier and much cheaper to change the shape of the hole (or program) than it is to try to make every Square Peg teen into something they are not (Round). It is an act of futility to keep trying to mold the teens all the time when a simple alteration to an existing program might serve more kids better overall.

Twenty

The Mythology of Adolescence

I think people should read fairy tales, because we're hungry
for a mythology that will speak to our fears.
Sandra Cisneros

Adolescence is a journey. It has always been the path from childhood to adulthood, and at a deeper level, adolescence is the gateway to manhood and womanhood. Adolescence is a process of personal and developmental growth, and for tens of thousands of years adults have sculpted and created clear paths for adolescents to navigate. It is the crossing place from dependency to responsibility.

Modern culture has all but eliminated most time-tested approaches, leaving current teens to navigate the turbulent waters of adolescence without the structured form of a map or guidance. Universally, almost every traditional culture came upon the same dynamics for working their adolescents; mostly the deliveries differed. It's critical to remember that they did this for a reason--millennia of trial and error led almost all cultures, often isolated from each other, to come to the same conclusion that adolescents need to be guided forward in a clear and specific way.

They did this through initiation practices, enduring and surviving rites of passage, and using the Hero's Journey that mythology expert Joseph Campbell synthesized out for us. Campbell broke down this elaborate system into three simple phases: Separation, Initiation, and Return. While Initiation, Rites of Passage, and the Hero's Journey seem to be synonymous, and they are certainly interrelated, they each have a distinct flavor to them similar to the difference between ceremony and ritual. A ritual is rite of celebration, often related to seasons of the year. A ceremony is the actual activity or behavior you do to celebrate the ritual. For example, the Fourth of July is a yearly ritual celebrating our independence. But one of the actual celebrations in this larger ritual is the shooting of fireworks.

On the path to adulthood, Initiation is the process of the trip, the need to move up and forward. It is the understanding that growth is up there, somewhere further ahead on the path. For example, a community has an initiation every year to test and promote youth into adulthood. There are ceremonies, gifts, and other practices related to the overall initiation in addition to the river challenge itself.

Challenge is the key ingredient in rites of passage, and risk is the key to growth. The physical challenge of crossing the river, facing one's fears, hopes and so on would be the Rite of Passage in this example or the ritual of yearly initiation. Finally, the *vessel* the youth would take to cross this river would be the Hero's Journey, the actual sequence of developmental changes and growth they go through along the way from preparing to completing then mentoring others.

Adolescence can be viewed in another mythological way, that of the labyrinth. As described earlier in this book, many, or most, people do not realize there is a distinct difference between a labyrinth and a maze. A maze is built to be confusing to the participant. Blind alleys and blocked paths confuse and confound the traveler, making this journey difficult and frustrating. Conversely, a labyrinth is a single guided path, allowing a clear direction to the center and back out again. Without the confusion and frustration of a maze, labyrinths offer a more subtle, internally focused trip where one learns from the quietness within.

Modern culture has created a scenario where adolescents are expected to get through the maze on their own. The maze is what happens when we look at adolescence as "a phase to get through." The maze creates anger and invites failure along the way, often leading the traveler nowhere at all. Getting stuck is common, which often leads to quitting. Quitting the path reflects quitting life.

Mythology expert Joseph Campbell noted shortly before his death that we in modern times are changing too fast to mythologize. In short, before our collective consciousness can create a new modern mythology (like the Greeks or Romans or even *Star Wars*) our culture has already moved on to something newer and we start again. In slower times, these reflections of our culture through stories and beliefs had time to evolve.

Indeed, try to think of a modern mythology most of us subscribe to. We have fantasy and sci-fi movies, a few strong groups of fanatic believers like Trekkies and role playing games, but these don't reach the cultural depth and acceptance to become a myth. They say good stories become legends become myths. We can't seem to get past mostly stories with a few occasional legends coming to light, but no one or nothing at a true mythological belief.

Adolescence has an often negative image in modern society, although this has certainly not always been the case. Historically, modern adolescent behavior is the exception rather than the rule. There's a reason so many independent and isolated communities all came across the same dynamics for helping their adolescents through this difficult coming of age period: it worked. Traditional, indigenous cultures did not have the luxury or resources for pursuing and embracing approaches that did not work in their favor. The universality of these approaches worldwide and historically is a clear indication of how well they worked and the necessity of providing them in the future.

ABOUT THE AUTHOR

Bret Stephenson M.A. is the author of *From Boys to Men: Spiritual Rites of Passage in an Indulgent Age* and *The Undercurrents of Adolescence: Tracking the Evolution of Modern Adolescence and Delinquency Through Classic Cinema.* He has been a counselor of at-risk and high-risk adolescents for almost 30 years. Bret has worked in residential treatment, clinical counseling agencies, group homes, private counseling, foster parent training, Independent Living Program, and managed mentoring and tutoring programs.

He has been a presenter and speaker at numerous national and international conferences and workshops, including being the teen coordinator at the International Transpersonal Association's Youth Conferences in America and Ireland, the United Nations World Peace Festival, Institute of Noetic Sciences and the World Children's Summit. Bret has worked with teens from more than 100 countries. As a men's group facilitator, he has also led workshops in the U.S. as well as Switzerland.

Bret is owner of the Adolescent Mind, a teen consulting business. He has trained and designed programs for numerous organizations including the Girl Scouts of America, Adirondack Leadership Expeditions and CASA. For the past five years Bret has been providing a number of workshops and lectures in Prague after the translated release of *From Boys to Men* in Czech.

www.adolescentmind.com
inquiries welcome

www.ingramcontent.com/pod-product-compliance
Lightning Source LLC
Chambersburg PA
CBHW072200280526
45788CB00002B/807